THE REAL MACBETH

&

Other Stories from Scottish History

D1113458

Maurice Fleming

THE REAL MACBETH

AND OTHER STORIES FROM SCOTTISH HISTORY

Illustrated by
ALYSON MACNEILL

THE MERCAT PRESS
EDINBURGH

First published in 1997 by Mercat Press
53 South Bridge, Edinburgh EH1 1YS

© Maurice Fleming, 1997
Illustrations © Alyson MacNeill, 1997

ISBN: 1873644 701

The publisher acknowledges subsidy from the Scottish Arts Council
towards the publication of this volume

Set in Ehrhardt at the Mercat Press
Printed and bound in Great Britain by
Redwood Books, Trowbridge, Wiltshire

Contents

Illustrations

Author's Note

I wish to thank Perth and Kinross Libraries for their unfailing help. Also my former colleague Alison Cook of *The Scots Magazine* whose knowledge of past issues saved much searching. Lastly, grateful thanks to Tom Johnstone of the Mercat Press for making it all such good fun.

Not everything in this book can be proved to be true. Some of the earlier stories in particular are impossible to verify. Nevertheless they have become part of Scotland's story through being told again and again. I have added nothing to them. They are as they have been passed down from one listener or reader to the next.

The Lost Battlefield

(AD 83)

O ne day a Roman writer called Tacitus sat down and wrote a story. It was a true story and he had heard it from an Army General who happened to be his wife's father. It told of a great battle the Romans had fought in a strange land far across the sea. The General had been in command and his side had triumphed.

The General's name was Agricola and he was very proud of his victory. Since his return to Rome he had received many honours and been praised as a hero. He was only too glad to tell his son-in-law of how cleverly he had outwitted and outfought the enemy.

Perhaps he exaggerated a little and perhaps Tacitus touched it up a bit, too, but still, the tale has a ring of truth and it's the first real story to come out of the mists of early Scotland. If Tacitus had not taken the trouble to write it down we would know little or nothing about it. Even as it is, a great mystery hangs over it, a mystery that still baffles today's experts.

Agricola had been sent to Britain to act as Governor. The Roman army had been in the southern half of the country for some years and most of it was well under control. Now Agricola turned his eyes north. He would not be content until he had conquered that part of the country too.

On his first expedition he got as far as the River Tay. He turned back then as he had other matters to deal with. Three years later he returned with a huge army determined to subdue the tribes who

1

lurked in the northern hills and forests.

The Romans called them the Caledonii, the Caledonians, and they were keen to get to grips with them. Naturally the Caledonians resented the advance of the strangers with their peculiar clothes and language, their foreign customs. They watched them from a distance as they marched in columns, setting up camps along the way. But they were in no hurry to face up to them in battle. They were content to bide their time.

The Romans knew the tribes were there. They felt all the time that they were being watched. It infuriated them that the Caledonians would not come out into the open and fight. Some of the soldiers grew anxious as they left the security of their southern forts further and further behind them. They felt cut off, surrounded by unseen enemies.

As for the tribes, they were growing ever more angered by the advance of the strangers. But which tribe was going to try to stop them? They could see that the Romans had many weapons. They had the air of a well-trained force. Most importantly the Roman army was large. According to Agricola he had several thousand foot soldiers and around 2,000 cavalry (horsemen). What tribe could stand up to all that? The answer was for the tribes to get together, to forget their inter-tribal quarrels and unite against the invaders.

First, they would need to elect a leader they could all trust, a man who had already proved himself in battle.

The man they chose was called Calgacus and he has the honour of being the first military leader recorded in our history. His name means The Swordsman, so we can take it that he was a formidable fighter as well as an inspiring leader.

He waited and watched the progress of the Romans before deciding where to confront them. The place he chose was the slope of a hill that faced a wide area of more even ground on which the Romans had set up a camp. The hill was called Mons Graupius.

Calgacus drew up his army—30,000 strong if Agricola is to be believed—in long ranks along the slope, most of them on a higher level than the Romans. They were nearly all foot-soldiers but some were in little pony-drawn carriages or chariots which were ready to carry spearsmen to different parts of the battlefield.

The Romans came out of their camp to face them, but before a blow was struck, the two leaders made speeches to inspire their men. Tacitus wrote these down as Agricola remembered them and they probably do capture the flavour of what the two leaders said.

Agricola reminded his troops of how they had been longing for this day. 'Often on the march,' he said, 'when you were tired of marshes, hills and rivers, I have heard the bravest of you ask, "when will we get a sight of the enemy? When will they come and fight us?" Well, now they have come. They have been flushed from their dens, and your prayers and courage will have an open field...Make this day the glorious crown of all these years of campaigning.'

You can imagine the cheers that rose at these words. But up on the hillside above them Calgacus was delivering an even better speech, one which is still quoted as one of the greatest battle speeches ever made.

He told the Caledonians, 'This remote land of ours, steeped in fable, has preserved us for this day. Now the furthest bounds of Britain have been laid waste and even the mystery of our isolation only whets the appetite of the invader. There are no tribes beyond us, nothing but bare rocks, the cruel sea, and, worse than these, the Romans, whose arrogance you will try in vain to escape...These men have pillaged the whole world, and now that their career of universal ruin has exhausted the land they take a toothcomb to the sea...'

He poured scorn on the Empire of which the Romans were so proud. 'Robbery, butchery, pillage—these are what they mean when they talk of "Empire".'

And then he used a phrase which has been famous ever since. The Romans, he said, 'make a desert and call it peace'.

He finished with the rousing call: 'As you go forward into the fight, look back to your ancestors and forward to those who will come after you.'

The tribesmen cheered, gripped their weapons and stood ready to fight.

Before Agricola gave the order to attack he ordered some of his men forward to lengthen his front line so that they were a more equal match for the long ranks of tribesmen facing them. Then the battle began.

At first both armies stood and hurled missiles at each other. Stones rained through the air from the slings both sides carried. It was the Caledonians who came off worst. Their shields were small and flimsy giving poor protection, while the Roman ones were big and strong. As many Caledonian heads streamed with blood the Romans began to advance, holding their shields high in front of them.

When they were close enough they drew their swords and with these, too, they had the advantage. Their swords had short, broad blades just two feet long—ideal for use in close combat. The tribesmen had large, heavy swords and while they were still trying to raise them above their heads, the Romans jabbed and slashed, inflicting terrible wounds.

The Romans were well protected by their helmets and their mail while the tribesmen wore very little and some preferred to fight completely naked. They were easily wounded and as they fell the crowded ranks behind them began to step backwards, colliding in turn with those behind them.

Seeing what was happening, Calgacus signalled to his charioteers waiting on the flanks. Each chariot was filled with spear-carrying warriors who now clung to the sides as the drivers lashed the ponies forward. It was a short journey to death. The Romans surrounded the spearsmen as they leaped from the chariots and they were quickly dealt with.

At one time the Romans had used chariots themselves, but they had lost too many men and discarded them. It amused them to see the Caledonians using what they looked on as out-of-date war vehicles.

They continued to battle their way forward, pushing the tribesmen back up the hillside. Desperately Calgacus sent a message to his troops at the very rear, furthest up the slope. He ordered them to fan out, pour down the hill and attack the Romans from their rear.

Seeing them coming, Agricola sent four regiments of cavalry to intercept them. The horsemen easily forced them to turn tail, then wheeled round and mounted the hill at the gallop to tackle the tribesmen from the back.

The Caledonians were now under attack at the front and rear. They were stumbling and falling over the bodies of their dead and wounded comrades and, to make matters worse, the ground further up the hill was rough and uneven.

Throwing down their weapons, many of the tribesmen started to make a run for it. They fled for cover to nearby woods, pursued by the Romans on foot and horseback. The countryside was soon littered with dead and dying.

Calgacus, who had begun the day with such a proud speech, is not heard of again. He is thought to have died on the field. Agricola claimed that 10,000 Caledonians fell and only 360 Roman lives were lost. These figures, however, may not be true: even in wars today it is often impossible to obtain accurate numbers of those killed in battle.

There had probably never been any real chance of a Caledonian victory. They were facing an experienced force hardened by years of tactical warfare. The Roman arms and equipment were in every way superior.

Never again did the tribes attempt to stand up to the power of Rome on any scale. All the evidence is that they learned to put up with the interlopers and even benefited from them through trading.

For Agricola, the battle of Mons Graupius (sometimes called Grampius) was a personal triumph for which he received high praise.

When he led his troops away from the scene he marched them through several tribal territories to impress and intimidate the inhabitants. He knew that news of his victory would have passed by word of mouth from one tribe to another. None of them would dare raise a finger to try to stop him.

As another display of strength he ordered ships of the Roman fleet to sail round the coast of Scotland on a celebration voyage.

Agricola probably expected that he would continue as Governor of Britain for some time, building more forts and strengthening the rule of Rome. However, not long after the Battle of Mons Graupius, Roman forces on the Danube were urgently in need of reinforcements. The troops in Scotland were ordered to go over and help. Agricola faced a fresh challenge.

Before they left, the Romans dismantled their forts and camps so that the local people could not make use of them. What could not be destroyed they buried in deep holes in the ground. Over 50 years were to pass before the Romans returned to invade this country again. The tribes had not forgotten the lesson Agricola had taught them and this time there was little opposition.

Although so much is known about the Battle of Mons Graupius, one vital piece of the story is missing.

Search any map of Scotland, new or old, and you will not find a hill of that name. This is the mystery that still puzzles historians. Where did the battle take place? Some of them argue for one hill, some for another.

Duncrub, in Strathearn, Perthshire, is the choice of one body of opinion. There was a temporary Roman camp at Dunning which would fit with the description of the site given by Tacitus. Craig Rossie in the same district is another suggestion.

Raedykes, near Stonehaven, is a favourite and so is Knock Hill, overlooking the Pass of Grange, east of Keith.

Around Blairgowrie, Perthshire, there is an old tradition that it was fought on the Moor of Cochrage above the town.

At the moment the most popular choice is Bennachie, the tall, peaked hill in Aberdeenshire. There was a camp near its base, and there is room on its lower slopes and in front of it for thousands of men to be drawn up in long ranks.

Excavations somewhere may one day provide the answer. Wherever Mons Graupius is, near it must lie the graves of thousands of those who died in the battle. Buried there also there will be broken chariots, discarded weapons and many other relics of the fight.

If ever all these are discovered, at Bennachie or another hill site, the mystery may be solved at last and the secret of 'Mons Graupius' revealed.

The Real Macbeth

(1040-1057)

William Shakespeare's play *Macbeth* tells the story of a man who becomes obsessed with ambition. Spurred on by his wife, Lady Macbeth, he kills the elderly King Duncan at Glamis Castle and becomes King himself.

Three witches have prophesied that this would happen, but they also said that it would be the descendants of his friend Banquo who would be the Kings of the future. To prevent this, Macbeth tries to kill Banquo's son but he escapes.

The witches then tell him to beware of the Thane of Fife, Macduff, but that he will suffer no harm until Birnam Wood comes to Dunsinane Hill—which sounds impossible. Macbeth attacks Macduff's castle and has Lady Macduff and her children slaughtered.

Macduff has joined forces with Duncan's son Malcolm and they now set out to stop Macbeth. Passing through Birnam Wood their troops cut branches off the trees and advance under their cover towards Dunsinane Hill, and so the prophecy comes true after all. Macbeth is killed and Malcolm proclaimed King. Lady Macbeth has already died insane.

It's a good story, but it has little to do with history. Shakespeare, it has to be remembered, did not sit down to write a history lesson. His aim was to entertain the audiences of the Globe Theatre, London. He also wanted to please the King of the time, James VI of Scotland, who, becoming King of England, too, had gone south to live in London. James liked to think that he was descended from Banquo and he also had a deep interest in witchcraft, so the scenes with the three witches were probably specially written to amuse him.

To get at the truth about Macbeth you have to forget most of what Shakespeare wrote about him. One thing is true, though: he did kill King Duncan and take his place on the throne. Duncan, however, was not the frail old man he is in the play, but quite a young man. And there is no evidence that Macbeth's wife played any part in the murder.

There *is* evidence, however, that Macbeth was in line to be King after Duncan and that he merely speeded up the process! People readily accepted him as their monarch after the crowning ceremony on the Stone of Destiny, at Scone, Perthshire.

Duncan had not been a popular King. He was headstrong and foolish. Against the advice of his advisors he had invaded Northumberland and attacked Durham. The adventure was a disaster and many Scots soldiers lost their lives.

People feared what Duncan might do next so there was relief rather than mourning when they heard he had met a sudden death.

Macbeth ruled firmly but fairly. It shows how stable things were that, around 1050, he was able to leave Scotland for several months and go on a pilgrimage to Rome. If he had been unpopular, there might well have been an uprising in his absence, but things went on as usual and he returned to a country that was quiet and at peace with herself.

It was not till a few years later that things went wrong for Macbeth. When King Duncan had died, he had left three young sons. The boys had been sent to different places for safety and the oldest one, Malcolm, had gone to England where he was brought up by the King, Edward the Confessor. Now the English encouraged Malcolm to avenge his father's death.

He returned to Scotland with an army headed by Siward, a Danish Earl well versed in the tactics of war. They marched right up to Perth and then to Dundee where reinforcements and supplies had arrived by ship and were waiting for them.

Soon afterwards Macbeth's army faced up to the invading force. Dunsinane Hill in the Sidlaws was probably where the battle took place. It is not a high hill: you can scramble up it in just a few minutes. On its flat summit are the remains of a fort. This has long been called Macbeth's Castle by local people and you can easily imagine him watching the enemy forces from its walls. The battle, though, took place out in the open, probably near the foot of the hill. The date was 27 July, 1054.

It was a long battle and many were killed. At its height it is said that members of Clan Menzies arrived to join Malcolm's side. On their way they had cut branches from rowan trees in Birnam Wood and carried them in the belief they would bring good luck. It is possible that Shakespeare heard about this and then invented the prophecy about Birnam Wood coming to Dunsinane Hill. It certainly makes good drama, even if it is not true.

Although Malcolm lost about 1,500 men, he won in the end and drove Macbeth and the remnants of the Scots army from the field.

Strangely, Malcolm did not at once follow up his victory. It may be that Edward the Confessor was not pleased by the heavy losses his army had suffered and did not want to risk losing any more. To keep Malcolm occupied he rewarded him by giving him Cumbria to rule and so for three years Macbeth was left undisturbed.

Then Malcolm went on the march again. Macbeth tried to rally forces behind him, but it seems that this time Malcolm was the more popular leader. His army grew while Macbeth's shrank. His supporters were deserting him daily. He fled north with just a handful of men. Malcolm made up on him at Queen's Hill, near Aboyne, and sent him running.

Malcolm caught up with him again at Lumphanan and this time Macbeth was slain while leading a last charge against his rival. His head was cut off and brought to Malcolm on a golden platter. It was a sad end to what had been, for those times, a long and successful reign.

And his wife? He had two. The second, Gruoch, already had a son, Lulach, and it was he who succeeded Macbeth. A few months later, he, too, was killed, and Malcolm at last became King of Scotland.

At Lumphanan you can see various features said to be connected with the battle. Local folk will tell you that Macbeth used the Peel of Lumphanan, a fort now covered under a green mound. Then there is Macbeth's Stone marking the spot where he died. There is also a spring from which he drank before the battle, and a cairn under which he is said to be buried. The truth is that his body was taken to Iona and lies there.

Macbeth, then, was not the power-crazed creature of Shakespeare's play, but a sound and level-headed ruler. The one black deed recorded against him, the murder of Duncan, proved his downfall. He was a very much better man than Duncan and made a better monarch, although one cannot blame Duncan's son Malcolm for his determination to avenge his father's early death.

The real Macbeth has been forgotten and his place taken by the fanciful character created by Shakespeare. But now *you* know the truth!

The People's Champion

(1270-1305)

On a hill near Stirling, visible for miles around, stands the Wallace Monument. Tall and proud, it was built over 500 years after the death of the man it celebrates: William Wallace.

Why did Scotland put up this Monument to a man who was long dead? Why is his name still remembered so well today?

He was a freedom-fighter, the greatest Scotland ever produced, and in the end he gave his life for his country, being put to death in a particularly horrible way.

He grew up at a time when Scotland was a very unhappy place to live. Edward I was determined that he was to be King of Scots as well as of England. He poured troops over the Border with orders to occupy towns, capture castles, and frighten the people into submission. Sadly, there were many Scots who were willing to go along with this, and even some who helped him to impose his rule. There always are such people in a situation like that.

The young William Wallace was not one of these. He bitterly resented the English soldiers who swaggered about the streets as if they owned the place. Their voices and their ill manners grated on him.

He is believed to have been born at Elderslie, near Paisley, and to have received most of his education in Dundee, but quite early in life his home was at Ayr.

One day, with a boy to carry his gear, he went fishing on the river Irvine. By late afternoon he had a full basket and was just leaving the riverbank when three English soldiers rode along. 'Oh, you've had a good catch,' said one of them. 'We'll take these. Hand them over.'

Wallace did not want an argument so he said, 'You can have half of them.'

The Englishman laughed and got off his horse. 'I'm taking them all. Come on—give me the basket.'

'You're not getting them,' said Wallace and the soldier's face changed.

'What?' he roared. Furious, he drew his sword.

Wallace had no weapon with him but he had his fishing-rod in his hand. He struck the man on the side of the head with the butt-end and he fell dead. The other two came at him, but Wallace grabbed the dead soldier's sword and fought them off, shouting to the boy to run for it. The soldiers soon saw Wallace was too much for them and they let him go.

That was only one of the encounters Wallace had with the English occupying troops. There are other stories of how he refused to be bullied. He was tall and strong and he learned to be skilful with the sword. Anyone rash enough to tackle him quickly realised that he had a dangerous opponent to deal with.

The Barns of Ayr

After killing the English soldier, Wallace had to go into hiding in the countryside near Ayr. While there he met other outlaws who shared his view that Scotland should be a free country and that it had as much right to rule itself as England did.

He became leader of a growing band of patriots who were set on making life difficult for the occupying troops.

One day word reached them of a terrible atrocity at Ayr. An English governor had been appointed for the town and he had decided to rid himself of some of the people he thought threatened his role.

He had invited leading members of several local families to meet him, saying he wanted to hold talks with them. The place was a group of large wooden buildings known as the Barns of Ayr.

The Governor made the invitation sound a friendly one and the men going along never dreamed they had anything to fear. They walked right into a trap.

As they arrived at the Barns in ones and twos they did not notice the ropes hanging from the beams, or if they did they thought nothing of it. But as soon as they were inside they were seized by soldiers who pushed their heads into a running noose which at once tightened, lifting them off their feet and strangling them. They all died in this way, their number including an uncle of William Wallace, a much-respected man who was Sheriff of Ayrshire.

Like everyone else Wallace was horrified when he heard the news. He was also very angry and determined the English would not go unpunished. He sent spies into Ayr to find out what was happening. In the evening they brought back word that the soldiers had been celebrating all day and were going to be sleeping that night in the Barns where the Scots had been murdered.

When it was dark Wallace led his men into Ayr. The English did not expect to be attacked, so no guards were on duty and the outlaws were able to creep up to the Barns and fasten the doors with ropes so that they could not be opened. They then piled straw against the wooden walls and set it alight.

As the fire took hold, the soldiers could be heard shouting and struggling to open the doors. It was no use. The few who did manage to escape the flames were cut down by the outlaws.

Another calamity befell the English that same night. Some of the troops had taken over rooms at a local Friary. The head Friar had heard of how the Scots had been tricked into walking into a death-trap. In the middle of the night he and his friars arose and attacked their unwelcome guests, killing many of them. This is remembered with bitter humour as the Friar of Ayr's Blessing.

These were cruel acts of revenge but you have to remember that this was a time when life was cheap and violence was commonplace.

Edward's Revenge

Wallace's campaign to rid Scotland of the English grew and spread. At the Battle of Stirling Bridge he won a famous victory and became the people's champion. Other successes followed but when Edward I himself came north, his army defeated Wallace and the great days were over.

Nevertheless, Wallace had lit a flame in Scottish hearts which burns to this day.

The story of his last weeks is tragic. Wallace had sent a message to Robert the Bruce asking him to take up the fight. He had been impressed by what he knew of Bruce, a younger man, and he believed that he could rouse the Scots to drive out the invaders.

The two men were to meet at a house at Robroyston, Glasgow. If that meeting had taken place, who knows what might have happened. Perhaps the two leaders would have worked together and gained Scotland her independence much sooner.

It was not to be. Amongst Wallace's supporters was a man called Sir John Menteith. Wallace did not know it but Menteith had been holding secret talks with the English and they had promised him rich rewards if he would help them to capture Wallace. Money had already changed hands and he was also offered a castle and other property.

As Wallace lay asleep in the house at night, Menteith hid his weapons and gave a silent signal to his own men. It is said that the signal was given in the kitchen by turning a loaf of bread upside down on the table. As soon as he did this, Menteith's men stormed the bedroom and bound Wallace's hands and feet, though not without a terrible struggle, for Wallace had the strength of a lion.

Menteith delivered his prisoner to Edward who carried him in triumph to London.

There he was taken before English judges at a trial in Westminster Hall.

A garland of leaves was placed around his neck as a mock reminder that Wallace had lived as an outlaw in the woods.

The trial was a travesty. A long list of Wallace's 'crimes' was read out to yells and jeers from the crowded courtroom. His request for a defence lawyer was refused.

When he was accused of treason against King Edward, Wallace shook his head defiantly. 'I could not be a traitor to Edward for I was never his subject.' He then told the court that in his eyes it was Edward who was the criminal and that he deserved to be hanged.

Menteith capturing Wallace

That was enough for the judges. Sentence was passed—the most cruel they could devise.

He was stripped naked, dragged through the streets behind a horse and thrashed all the way with sticks and belts while stones and garbage were flung at him.

By the time he reached the gallows Wallace was half-dead and had to be supported so that the rope could be put around his neck. He was pushed into space but before he could die he was taken off again so that he could be mutilated with a knife while still alive.

Finally his body was chopped into pieces and his limbs sent to different parts of the country for public display. Newcastle, Berwick-on-Tweed, Stirling and Perth all received an arm or a leg. His head was placed on Tower Bridge in London.

So died a great national hero. His brave story is told at the Wallace Monument and there are statues of him at Edinburgh Castle, Aberdeen, Lanark, near Dryburgh in the Borders and elsewhere.

Scotland will never forget its people's champion.

Bruce, the Hero-king
(1274-1329)

After the death of Sir William Wallace, Scotland's future as an independent country seemed doomed. With him out of the way, Edward I believed there would be little real opposition to his rule.

He was wrong. At that moment there stepped onto the stage a new leader.

In several ways, Robert the Bruce, Earl of Carrick, was an unlikely successor to Wallace. Although born at Turnberry Castle in Ayrshire, he was of Anglo-Norman blood. He had fought for Edward, even sworn homage to him, and those who knew him said he was rash, quick-tempered, and too fond of having a good time.

Bruce was rich and could afford to live in style. He owned lands in Scotland, an estate in England, a house in London and a manor in Tottenham.

Yet he chose to turn rebel and devote his life to defending Scotland against English aggression.

His greatest hour was to be on the field of Bannockburn, the most inspiring victory in all Scots history, but countless other tales are told of him, for he had many adventures, and suffered setbacks and disappointments as well as triumphs on the long road to national freedom.

There follow just some of the stories that have come down to us.

The Death of the Red Comyn

When a great leader dies, people watch and wonder, who is to take over? When Wallace was cruelly killed, some pointed to John Comyn and said 'He is the man'.

The Red Comyn of Badenoch belonged to a powerful family and he had friends who could provide men and arms.

Like Bruce, John Comyn owned lands in Scotland and England and, like Bruce again, he had for a time supported Edward. Bruce and he had once quarrelled violently when Bruce had accused him of betraying secret resistance plans to the English. Now, though, Bruce and Comyn both felt it was time to bury their differences.

The two men arranged to meet at Greyfriars' church in Dumfries. Neither had any liking for the other yet they felt they must work together for their country's sake. They greeted each other warmly enough and wandered down to the altar where they could talk unheard.

No-one knows exactly what they discussed for Bruce never disclosed it. It is likely, though, that Bruce told Comyn that he had his eyes on the Scottish crown and that Comyn scoffed at this. Perhaps Comyn made it clear that he wanted it for himself.

Whatever the cause, their voices rose in furious argument. It ended with Bruce drawing his dagger and plunging it into his rival's body. John Comyn fell to the floor in front of the altar. With the dripping dagger still in his hand, Bruce hurried from the church and joined his waiting followers. 'I fear I have slain the Red Comyn,' he gasped.

One of his friends, Sir Roger de Kirkpatrick, drew his sword. 'I'll mak siccar,' he said grimly ('I'll make sure'). With another man he rushed into the church and completed the murder.

As they all galloped away from the church, Bruce was appalled at what he had done. To have killed someone so well-known was bad enough. To have done it in a church, in front of the altar, was going to shock many.

It did. To those who had said Bruce was too hot-tempered to be a leader, this seemed proof positive. He made many enemies that day, for the Red Comyn's family and friends could not forgive Bruce. Many Scots who might have supported his bid for the throne refused now to do so, some believing that Bruce had deliberately lured Comyn to Dumfries in order to kill him.

When the Pope in Rome heard of the murder, he had Bruce excommunicated—expelled from the Church.

Yet despite this huge setback, six weeks later, on 25 March 1306, Robert the Bruce was crowned King at Scone Abbey in the presence of four bishops, five earls and a great crowd of friends and followers from all over the country. He had made the worst possible start to his campaign with the callous murder of John Comyn, but already enough Scots trusted him and believed that he was Scotland's only hope of fighting off 'proud Edward's power'.

The Brooch of Lorn

Bruce had been crowned King, but across the Border, in England, Edward was determined that his reign would be short. Not long after the coronation an English force scattered Bruce's men at Methven, Perthshire, and he had to keep on the move with a small company of faithful soldiers, relatives and friends.

Retreating into the Highlands they strayed onto lands owned by MacDougall of Lorn, a cousin of the Red Comyn. MacDougall saw this as his chance to avenge his cousin's death.

Near Tyndrum he set an ambush for the royal party. As they broke out of it Bruce divided his company into three and sent them off in different directions. He knew it was him MacDougall wanted to capture and he hoped to confuse him.

To his surprise MacDougall's men did not hesitate. They followed his own party and ignored the others. Bruce divided his group again, but it made no difference. They kept hard on his trail.

Again Bruce split up the group and in the end he was alone with only one companion. Still the MacDougalls followed.

When they caught up with him Bruce saw the reason why. A dog he had once owned came bounding towards him and jumped up to lick his hand. The MacDougalls had captured it and used it to betray its master by following his scent.

The MacDougall chief gave a signal for five of his best men to close in on Bruce. With his one companion Bruce fought them off and they fell one by one.

It was a desperate fight and in the melee Bruce's plaid was torn off along with a favourite brooch that held it. He had to leave them lying on the ground while he and his friend made their escape.

Exhausted, they came to a stream and lay down to rest, but it was not long before they heard, once again, the clash of steel and the dog barking eagerly as it sought its master. Urging his friend to follow him, Bruce stepped into the water, waded downstream and came out on the other side.

The dog reached the burn, waded across and ran up and down the bank trying to pick up the scent. Bruce, now some distance away, heard its disappointed yelps as it searched in vain.

Bruce never forgot how the MacDougalls had hunted him like an animal and later, when he was in a position to do so, he punished the clan for what they had done.

The brooch he dropped that day was picked up and kept in the MacDougall family, eventually becoming a treasured heirloom. It has long been known as the Brooch of Lorn.

Bruce and the Spider

King Robert the Bruce sat in a cave on the Isle of Arran, a disappointed man. He had been hunted off the mainland by King Edward's troops—and not all of them English, for some Scots had turned against Bruce and wanted to see him captured and killed. It was only a few months since he had been crowned at Scone, but that great day now seemed a very long time ago, almost like a dream.

Early in his campaign he had sent his Queen, daughter Marjorie and sister Mary northwards under the protection of his brother Neil. He had prayed they would find a place of safety and they thought they had found one in Kildrummy Castle, near Alford, Aberdeenshire.

The English discovered they were there and laid siege to the castle, but those inside had plenty of supplies and were confident they could hold out. However, there was a traitor in their midst. The English had promised the blacksmith in the castle that they would give him as much gold as he could carry away if he would help them take the castle.

The smith, a man called Osbarn, heated the blade of a plough till it was red-hot and then threw it in the grain-store. The grain caught fire and the smoke and flames destroyed the food stores.

The garrison surrendered but when Osbarn went to claim his reward, the English laughed, seized him and poured melted gold down his throat.

Neil Bruce was beheaded and two of the women were treated by Edward in a particularly cruel way. Bruce's sister Mary, who had been very outspoken against Edward, was taken to Roxburgh Castle and locked in a cage constructed of wood and iron. The Countess of Buchan, who had taken part in the coronation ceremony, was placed in a similar cage in the tower of Berwick Castle. They were kept in the cages for several years.

Edward had at first ordered that Marjorie, Bruce's daughter, then about 11, should also be caged. She was to be taken to the Tower of London and kept there and no-one was to be allowed to speak to her. However, he was persuaded to withdraw the order and he sent her to a nunnery instead.

All this was on Bruce's mind as he lay in the cave on Arran. He felt he had brought nothing but trouble and sorrow to his family and he was getting nowhere with his plan to muster support for a Scottish stand against Edward. Perhaps, he thought, the time had come to give up.

He had always wanted, one day, to fight in the Crusades in the Holy Land. Maybe now he should do so and gain forgiveness for the murder of the Red Comyn.

As he lay there his eye was caught by a spider on the roof of the cave. It had spun a long thread and was trying to swing it to reach the wall. Six times it tried and six times it failed.

'Now.' Bruce said to himself, 'if it gives up I will give up too and go to the wars in Palestine. But if it tries once more and succeeds, then I will try again.'

He held his breath as he watched the spider. For a long moment it hung motionless and then, with a great effort, it swung the thread to the wall and landed on it. It had succeeded.

Bruce leaped to his feet. He would fight on. He would not give up.

He left the island, returned to the mainland and began to gather support around him. It was to be some time before the tide turned, but turn it did. Edward I died and his son, also Edward, became King of England and continued the campaign to subjugate the Scots.

In 1314 Edward himself came to Scotland at the head of an army far larger than Bruce could hope to raise. The two sides came face to face on marshy ground by the Bannock Burn, near Stirling. Against all the odds the Scots won and from that day Scotland's future was assured and Bruce became the Hero King.

He had inspired his men to victory and his battle tactics were brilliant. Yet it might have gone terribly wrong for him right at the start. As the English began their advance on the Scots, who were waiting in trenches, one of Edward's knights, Sir Henry de Bohun, saw Bruce riding along the line on a garron giving his soldiers a few words of encouragement. He had not yet put on his armour.

Fully armoured, de Bohun raised his lance, spurred his horse into a charge and headed straight for Bruce. Fortunately, Bruce had his battleaxe. He waited until de Bohun reached him and then, rising in his saddle, he brought the axe down with a crash, splitting the knight's helmet and head. To a great cheer from his men, Bruce then rode off to put on his armour.

There is an excellent Visitor Centre at Bannockburn which shows how the battle was fought. The Centre is well worth seeing as is the fine statue of Bruce wielding his famous battleaxe. Bruce assembled his troops here and the battle took place about a mile to the east on low-lying marshland that has long since been drained and altered. For every Scot, though, this is hallowed ground.

The old song 'Scots Wha Hae' is based on Bruce's words to his army before the battle. It was written by Robert Burns and captures the determination of the man as he encouraged his troops to give of their all. The last verse is:

> Lay the proud usurpers low!
> Tyrants fall in every foe!
> Liberty's in every blow!
> Let us do or die!

Many people think this great song of freedom should be Scotland's national anthem.

The Declaration of Arbroath

Scots during Bruce's reign were always aware that their country's independence was under threat. Even after Bannockburn, Edward still did not stop scheming against Scotland.

Unfortunately the Pope listened more to him than he did to Bruce and he refused to recognise Bruce as King or to lift the excommunication order he had placed on him. This was a serious matter, for the Pope was more powerful than he is now. It was harmful to Scotland's relations with other countries and the Scots people felt not only insulted but insecure about the future.

That was why, in 1320, a letter was drawn up and sent to the Pope on behalf of all the people of Scotland. It was signed by nobles, bishops and many others representing ordinary folk and it has become known as the Declaration of Independence or the Declaration of Arbroath.

It told the Pope how Scots had always valued their freedom, how Edward I had invaded their country and how Bruce had rescued them from tyranny.

The Declaration makes it clear that in Scotland power belongs to the people and not to kings or governments and it underlines this by stating that, while they respected Bruce as their leader, 'Yet if he should give up what he has begun, and agree to make us and our kingdom subject to the King of England or the English, we should exert ourselves at once to drive him out as our enemy and a subverter of his own rights and ours, and make some other man our King.'

Then comes the most famous passage of all:

'For as long as but one hundred of us remain alive, never will we on any conditions be brought under English rule. It is in truth not for glory, nor riches, nor honours that we are fighting, but for freedom—for that alone, which no honest man gives up but with his life.'

This Declaration is the most precious item in Scotland's archives. It was written in Latin so translations of it sometimes differ slightly but nothing can take away from its powerful message or the wonderful phrases in which it is expressed. The American Declaration of Independence is based on it.

It was fitting that this document was drawn up during the reign of King Robert the Bruce, the greatest leader in our history.

Black Agnes

(1338)

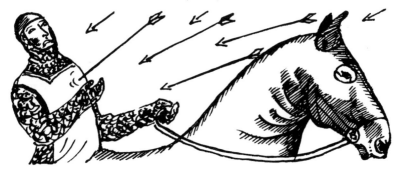

There is not much left of the once proud castle of Dunbar: just a few craggy remains near the harbour of this old East Lothian fishing town. I use the word proud because everybody in Dunbar was once very proud of the castle and of the woman who held an army at bay for six long months.

It was 1338 and her husband, the Earl of March and Dunbar, was away fighting the English. In his absence he had left his wife Agnes in charge of the castle, which was under siege. Black Agnes—she got that name because of her dark hair and swarthy skin—could see the English troops ranged outside the castle walls. They were set on capturing it and she was determined to keep them out.

Fortunately there was only one main entrance from the beach and it was narrow and easily guarded. The only other way in was at the back, by sea, and it, too, could be kept under constant watch and any intruder speedily dealt with.

Commanding the English troops was Montague, Earl of Salisbury, and he was furious at not being able to take the castle—especially since a woman was in charge of it! He brought along a newfangled device for throwing large stones at the outside walls. It was trundled near to the wall and then, time and again, stones from it were flung through the air to crash against the stonework. Every time they did so, Black Agnes and her maids would appear on the battlements

25

with clean towels in their hands and they would lean over and wipe the wall where the stones had struck, mocking the men below.

This drove Montague wild with anger. He sent for another new device, a sort of shed on wheels. Two men went inside the shed and it was rolled up to the foot of the walls. Being under cover they could not be hit by arrows from the defenders and they at once started to hammer a hole in the wall with pickaxes and mining tools.

Up on the battlements, Black Agnes made a signal to her men. A huge stone was pushed over the parapet and landed with a crash on the roof of the shed, smashing it to fragments and scattering the men inside.

After that, Montague had to admit to himself that he would just have to sit it out and wait until there was no food left in the castle. Then, he thought, they will have to surrender and let us in.

One day, he rode quite close to the wall with one of his knights. Both were well protected against a possible stray arrow from the castle, but the knight felt particularly safe. He was wearing three folds of mail over a thick leather jacket.

They were laughing and chatting as they rode by when suddenly an arrow flew from the battlements. It had been fired with such force that it penetrated right to the knight's heart and he fell dead on the spot.

As Montague spurred his horse away, he was heard to remark dryly, 'That must be one of my lady's love tokens. Black Agnes's love-shafts pierce to the heart!'

A few nights later, Montague was told that one of Black Agnes's staff wanted to see him. He told his soldiers to bring him in. The servant told him he was tired of the siege. He wanted it finished with. If Montague and a small party of his best soldiers came to the gate the following night, he would arrange for it to be open and the portcullis up. Montague and his men could then rush in and take the garrison by surprise.

Montague rubbed his hands in glee. The following night he moved towards the castle with a group of handpicked soldiers. Stopping a little way from it he peered into the darkness. Yes, the gate was open and the portcullis raised! He gave a signal and led the little party forward cautiously. But one of his officers, a Northumberland squire, was impatient. He rushed forward and through the gate. No sooner was he behind the portcullis than it clanged down behind him, trapping him inside.

It was all a trick of Black Agnes's. She had sent the servant to see Montague and had hoped to capture him. She very nearly had. Not long after that Montague could only watch helplessly from the shore as a ship sailed up close to the castle's sea entrance and unloaded supplies of fresh provisions. He knew then that his task was hopeless. He had already waited for many weeks and he could not sit there twiddling his thumbs any longer.

The following day, Black Agnes, her maids and soldiers watched from the battlements and windows and cheered as they saw Montague's army packing up and riding off. Agnes was the toast of the garrison and of all Scotland.

Kate Bar-the-Door

(1437)

When James I rode out of Edinburgh Castle to go and spend Christmas in Perth he little thought he was riding to his death. None of his courtiers had dared tell him of the warning signs.

The night he had decided to go to Perth, a fiery sword had been seen suspended in the sky above the Castle, and later it had been sighted hovering above St Johnstone, as Perth was then called. On the same night a calf had been born with a horse's head. These were taken as bad omens by his superstitious followers.

Now, as they neared the ferry over the Forth, the King's horse reared and shied. An old woman had risen from a stone by the wayside and seized the horse's bridle. Her ragged clothes and long hair blew in the wind as she stared up into James's face.

'Get out of the way, woman!' the courtiers shouted, but she was going to have her say.

'Gin ye cross that ferry,' she said, 'ye'll ne'er cross back again!'

James laughed, tugged the bridle from her hand and rode on. Behind him his retainers looked at one another and shook their heads. It was another ill omen.

They knew they would be wasting their time trying to persuade James to heed her warning. Since he had become King, he had seemed fearless of all dangers. Well educated, fond of poetry and music, he was also a skilled archer and a keen sportsman. It seemed that everything he tackled he did well.

He had set out, at the start of his reign, to rid Scotland of its most troublesome nobles, ambitious men who fought amongst themselves, oppressed their tenants and schemed against him. His campaign had been a success. Scotland was now a far better and safer country to live in.

He had won the support of the people, who felt he was on their

28

side and warmed to his outgoing personality. They believed he was a fair and honest ruler.

But, of course, he had made enemies amongst the nobles whom he had cut down to size, and bitterest of them all was Sir Robert Graham. The King thought he had taught Graham a lesson when he had sent him to prison for a spell and that he had curbed his lust for power by taking from him the old family lands in Strathearn. He did not realise the hatred that seethed in Graham, a hatred that was now coming to the boil.

The King was in high spirits when he arrived at the monastery in Perth where he was to stay. His Queen, Joan, was already there with her ladies-in-waiting, among them a young girl, Katherine Douglas, who was devoted to James and her royal mistress.

Blackfriars Monastery was a fine old building that looked across the Tay to the green, wooded slopes of Kinnoull Hill. Despite its size it was not big enough to house all of James's court and some of his retainers had been found lodgings in rooms in the town.

It was unfortunate that the Monastery stood just outside the town walls because it meant that those staying in the town had to be in their rooms by curfew every night when the town gates closed. They were then cut off from the royal party till morning.

If this worried some of James's party it did not worry him. He was set on enjoying himself during his stay and nothing was going to stop him. During the day he played tennis and other games and in the evenings he joined in chess or draughts and listened to music on the harp or the pipes. He was a singer and musician himself so he could join in with the best of them.

Christmas passed, and all January, and it was well into February. James and Queen Joan showed no thoughts of returning to Edinburgh. Why should they? He had declared St Johnstone to be Scotland's capital. All it lacked was a palace or castle for him to live in. Until one was built, the Monastery suited him well enough.

One night there came a hammering at the door. When a servant opened it, an old woman pushed past him. 'Oh, sir,' she pleaded, 'I maun see the King!'

It was the woman who had tried to warn him at the ferry and she was dirtier and more ragged than ever.

The servant pushed away the grimy hand that seized his arm. He told her it was impossible to see the King who was enjoying an evening's entertainment with his friends.

She wrung her hands and appealed to him. 'Let me see him— afore it's ower late.'

Reluctantly the servant went to the King and told him about his visitor. James might have granted her a few minutes but some of his courtiers, for reasons of their own, told him he should send her away. The servant went back and and told her. He never forgot the look in her eyes as she went out into the night.

Soon afterwards, the Queen went to her room accompanied by Katherine Douglas and her other ladies-in-waiting. They were laughing as they recalled some of the harmless fun of the evening. A little later James joined them to say goodnight. As he warmed his hands at the fire they all heard from outside the sound of horses' hooves and the ring of armour. Rushing to the window they saw horsemen carrying blazing torches to light the way in the dark. At once they suspected the worst.

The Monastery was surrounded by a moat and all the entrances were locked at night, so it should have been quite safe inside. It was not. Planks of wood had been stretched across the water and the horsemen had dismounted and were coming over. The doors swung open to their touch, for they had been unlocked by someone on the inside.

Once in the building the intruders had to pass through other doors before they could reach the royal chambers. All should have been lockfast, but friends of the conspirators had done their work well. All the doors opened as the invaders tramped through the corridors. They were led by Sir Robert Graham himself. When a young page-boy stood in his way he cut him down with his sword.

The King knew it was him they were after and that his only hope was escape. He ran to the window but it was heavily barred and he could not get out that way. Suddenly he remembered that below the room was a tiny cellar with a hole in the wall leading out to the tennis courts. It was his only chance. He rushed to the fireplace, grabbed the coal tongs and prised up the floorboards. As soon as he dropped into the cellar, Katherine and the others pressed the boards back in place.

The footsteps were thundering closer. Katherine ran to the door. There should have been a large bar or bolt that could be slid along to secure it, but to her dismay it had gone. Not hesitating she thrust an arm through the hasp where the bolt should have gone and stood with her back to the door. Next moment it crashed open, breaking her slender arm.

Graham and his men filled the room. They were armed with swords, axes and other weapons and they ransacked the chamber, turning over the furniture in search of James. They were puzzled and angry because they had been sure he was there, but at last they rushed out to look in other parts of the Monastery.

As their footsteps died away, the ladies raised the floorboards. When James had gone down into the cellar he had intended to crawl outside through the narrow hole that led to the tennis court. To his horror he found it had been blocked up and he remembered that he himself had given the order for this to be done because, when he was playing tennis, the balls sometimes rolled into it and were lost.

He was about to climb back up into the room when the tramp of feet was again heard approaching along the corridor. The ladies had just time to push back the boards when the assassins again filled the room. One of them, who knew the building well, had remembered about the cellar.

He found the loose floorboards and tore them up. Another man, Sir John Hall, dropped inside and saw the King crouching in the shadows. He advanced on him with a knife in his hand, but James, who was fitter than his attacker, leaped at him, gripped him by the throat and threw him to the ground. A second man descended and got the same treatment.

Up in the room Sir Robert Graham pushed the others aside. Leaping down into the cellar he raised his sword over the unarmed

King. A few terrible strokes and it was all over.

So died James the First, a ruler who had done much for Scotland during his short reign and could have done so much more.

James was buried at Perth. Joan, his widow, had all his killers hunted down and put to death. None of them was spared.

Katherine Douglas was ever after known as Kate Bar-lass or Kate Bar-the-Door on account of her brave act in trying to hold the door to save her King.

Escape!

(1479)

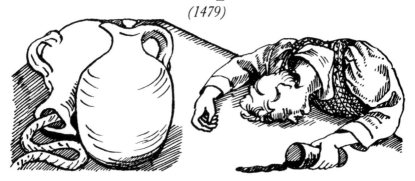

James III did not trust anybody. Most of all he did not trust his two brothers the Duke of Albany and the Earl of Mar. So when his Flemish astrologer and local 'witches' all warned him against danger from within his own family, he felt that his suspicions were justified.

He had his brothers arrested on charges of treason. Mar was imprisoned in the Edinburgh Tolbooth where he died mysteriously. Some said he was hacked to death in his bath.

That left Albany. Good looking, able, 20 years of age, he was the person the King feared most. Perhaps he felt that in many people's eyes Albany would make a better king than the one they had. James had him brought to Edinburgh Castle and locked in a cell. Then he ordered his execution. In his fine apartment within the Castle, James sat rubbing his hands in satisfaction. He was well pleased with the way he had handled the whole matter. One brother was dead and the other would soon join him.

Meantime, in his cell Albany was receiving a surprise present. A well-wisher had sent him two large flasks of wine. One was indeed full of wine, but the other contained a rope and a message. Unfolding the parchment Albany read that the wine was from a French ship docked at Leith. If with the rope's help he could escape, a passage was booked for him when the ship left for France.

Albany went to the window of his cell and looked out. He was on

Albany escaping with his servant

the north side, the side now facing Princes Street, and far in the distance, beyond the woods and moorland he could see the Firth of Forth flowing down to the open sea...

He called for his servant and they had a long talk. Both knew there was no time to waste, for the next day had been set for Albany's execution.

That evening the servant went to the Captain of the Guard with an invitation from his master. Would the Captain care to sample a little French wine? The Captain was easily persuaded. Albany re-filled his tankard again and again till the Captain grew drowsy and fell asleep. Then Albany threw the rope over the window and down the cliff-face.

'You go first,' he told his servant. Hand over hand the servant made his way down in the darkness. Alas, the rope was not long enough to reach the ground. He fell the final stretch and broke a hip.

Before he climbed down, Albany extended the rope by tying his sheets to it. He reached the ground safely. His servant was unable to walk so Albany flung him over his shoulder and carried him all the way to Leith.

It was morning before a watchman spotted the rope dangling over the Castle rock. Rushing to the cell they found the Captain of the Guard just wakening from his drunken sleep.

The news was swiftly carried to the King who would not believe it until he had seen the empty cell for himself.

By that time the French vessel was out of the Forth and on her way to France. Albany and his servant were aboard her, celebrating their escape with another flask of the best French wine.

'Archibald Bell-the-Cat'

(1482)

One by one a group of men gathered in Lauder Church. When everybody had arrived, they closed and locked the door. All of them belonged to what had been the most powerful families in Scotland. Their fathers and grandfathers had been close to the throne, advising the King of the time and receiving favours in return.

Recently, things had been very different. James III preferred very different company. His favourites were artists, musicians, architects, astrologers. Even his tailor saw more of him now than any of his nobles. He had several particularly close friends and they had formed a sort of council, giving the King their views and opinions on all sorts of matters.

The nobles had had enough of it. Today they were meeting in this Borders church to decide a course of action.

They talked for hours, growing angrier and angrier. All sorts of plans were suggested, but at the end of it all there seemed only one thing to do. The King would have to be told of their feelings.

'It's the only way,' a senior noble said. 'One of us must go to him and demand that he disband this council and listen to us instead.'

There was a chorus of agreement, but then came the question: who was to tell the King? Whoever it was, he was likely to get a very unfriendly reception! As they all looked at the floor or out of the window one of the wiser heads among them, Lord Gray, compared their dilemma to a household of mice plagued by a cat.

'The mice,' he said, 'know that if they hang a bell round the cat's neck they will all be safe because they will hear it coming and can run to safety. The trouble is none of them is willing to risk its life by going near enough the cat to put the bell round its neck!'

After he had spoken there was silence and then one of their

number rose to his feet. 'I will bell the cat,' he said.

He was one of the youngest present and his name was Archibald Douglas, Earl of Angus.

As the others breathed a sigh of relief he said he would go immediately to see the King who was camped in the vicinity. 'Wait here until I return,' he told them.

He was back sooner than they expected and his grim face warned them he did not bring good news. He told them he had pleaded with the King to abolish the council but it had been no use. James would not listen.

As the nobles sat fuming, there was a knock on the church door. When one of them opened it in strutted one of James's special favourites, an architect called Cochrane. Of all James's new friends he was the one the nobles most disliked because of his airs and graces. He always dressed better than any of them. Today he was attired in black velvet and gold, with a golden chain. A gold-tipped horn hung at his side.

He sauntered down the aisle and asked what the meeting was about. 'Why was I not told about it?' he enquired.

The nobles closed in around him. Archibald Douglas snatched off the gold chain. 'A rope will suit you better,' he said.

Cochrane was taken aback.

'My Lords, is this jest or earnest?' he exclaimed as they pushed and jostled him.

He soon knew the answer. He was held prisoner while some of the nobles, now properly roused, set off and rounded up other leading members of the council.

A sort of mock trial was held at which the nobles accused their prisoners of misleading the King and interfering in the affairs of the country. They found them all guilty, condemned them to death and had them hung from Lauder Bridge. They then took the King prisoner and escorted him to Edinburgh under armed guard. For a time he was locked in a cell in the Castle but word of this leaked out and there were rumblings of unrest in the country.

His gaolers released him, but if they thought that James had learned his lesson, they were mistaken. Some of his old favourites remained and he found new ones whom he preferred to his nobles.

Amongst the men who had been hanged from the bridge were some brilliant minds. Cochrane, for instance, for all his fancy clothes and foppish manners, was a talented architect responsible, among other things, for the Great Hall of Stirling Castle, still a splendid sight today.

For his part in the matter Archibald Douglas earned himself a nickname which has come down in the history books. His friends called him 'Archibald Bell-The-Cat', and that is how he is remembered.

The Gudeman o' Ballengeich

(1512-1542)

James V sat brooding in Holyrood Palace. He thought he was doing his best for his country but did his subjects agree? How did ordinary people live? What sort of problems did they have? Longing to find out he hit on an idea. He would dress himself in ordinary clothes, take a staff in his hand and go walking through the streets and out into the countryside. He would mix with people in ale houses and at markets, ask their opinion on things—especially what they thought of their King! So that is what he did. Every now and again he would lay aside his fine clothes and, dressed as a poor man, he would slip out through a back door of the Palace and disappear for two or three days or more.

Sometimes folk he spoke to would ask him who he was. 'Oh,' he would say, 'I'm the Gudeman o' Ballengeich.' A gudeman in those days was simply a farm tenant and Ballengeich was a croft near Stirling. Why he chose that name we don't know, but it worked because everybody he met seemed to accept it without question.

We don't know all the adventures he had, but here are two of them...

The first took place at Cramond. It's part of Edinburgh now but at that time it was several miles outside the city. He was making his way back to Holyrood when he was attacked by thieves, or muggers as we would call them now. There were four or five of them and he would not have had much of a chance against them except that he was close to the bridge over the river Almond. The bridge was high and narrow and just wide enough for one person to cross at a time. Standing on it he fended off his attackers with his staff. They were determined and it was all he could do to keep them at bay. Desperately he began to wonder how long he could continue to hold them off.

Near the bridge was a little farm called Braehead and its tenant, John Howieson, was working in his barn when he heard the commotion. He was threshing corn with a flail, a hand implement, and he stepped out to see what was happening.

Seeing one man being attacked by a gang of scoundrels he did not hesitate. He still held his flail in his hand and he rushed over and began to strike out at them.

A few hearty blows drove the robbers back. Like most thieves they were cowards at heart. They gave up and ran off throwing curses over their shoulders as they went.

He then helped the stranger over to his barn and sat him down. He fetched him a ewer (jug) of water and a basin and helped him to wash the bruises on his face and hands.

Soon James felt refreshed enough to continue his journey, but John would not let him go alone. He insisted on walking some way with him in case the thieves were lying in wait, ready to pounce again. Before the two men parted, James shook his hand warmly and asked him his name.

'John Howieson of Braehead.' He explained that he was a miller and that the farm did not belong to him but to the King.

'And what would be your dearest wish, John Howieson?'

'Oh, that's easy,' said John. 'I would be the happiest man in Scotland if I owned Braehead Farm.' He looked at James curiously. 'You haven't told me *your* name.'

'I'm the Gudeman o' Ballengeich,' said James. 'I work at the Palace of Holyrood. How would you like to see over it?'

'Oh, yes!' said John.

'Then come on Sunday. I'll show you round. That will be my way of thanking you for what you have done for me today.'

The fight on the bridge

And so it was arranged. On the Sunday John put on his best clothes and set off for Edinburgh. When he reached the gates of Holyrood he asked for the Gudeman o' Ballengeich. James had left word with the sentries that he was to be told as soon as John arrived. Now he came out and greeted John, dressed as he had been on the day they had met.

As promised, he took John on a tour of the building. The miller had never seen anything like it before and he was full of wonder as he was shown one splendid room after another.

'And now,' said James at last, 'how would you like to see the King?'

'Oh,' said John, 'I'd love to—if you're sure the King won't be angry?'

'No, no,' smiled James. 'I promise you he won't be angry.'

He told John that the King would be with his nobles in the Great Hall. There would be a lot of people around him.

'And how will I know which is the King?' asked John, 'for I have never seen him before.'

'That will be easy,' James assured him. 'They will all have their heads bare except the King. He will be the only one in the room wearing a bonnet.'

They walked into the Great Hall. It was crowded as James had said. John stared around. 'But which is the King?' he whispered.

'Didn't I tell you he would be the one wearing the bonnet?'

'Then,' said John, 'it must be either you or me for all but us two are bare-headed!'

James burst out laughing and admitted that he was indeed King James. Poor John didn't know where to look or what to do, but James put him at his ease.

'I have brought you here,' he said, 'so that I can reward you for coming to my aid.' He reminded John that he had said he would be the happiest man in Scotland if only he owned Braehead Farm. 'It's yours,' he said.

John started to thank him but James interrupted. 'There's one condition,' he said.

'What's that, your Highness?' asked John nervously.

The King smiled. 'That you and your heirs will always be ready to provide a ewer and basin so that your monarch can wash his hands when passing through Cramond.' John sank to his knees and gave his solemn promise that the condition would be kept.

And so it was. A descendant of John Howieson offered a ewer of water and a basin to King George IV 200 years later in 1822. In 1842 the same was done for Queen Victoria, and again in 1927 for George III and in 1952 for Queen Elizabeth.

There is still a bridge over the Almond. It's not the one James stood on, but it is on the same spot and you can stand on it today and think of that time when he stood there and, with the miller's help, fought off the thieves. Braehead Farm is no longer there, but that is not to say that there may not be one or two of John Howieson's descendants still in the district, ready to provide a basin and ewer of fresh water if ever a royal request is made for it!

Just like the Royal Family today, James V had more than one residence.

This story took place in and around Stirling because he was at Stirling Castle at the time.

He had a number of guests staying and he wanted them to taste the local venison, so he ordered some of his men to go up to the Ochil Hills and kill some deer. The hunting party set off and before nightfall they had killed several fine beasts. They slung the dead animals over their horses' backs and turned towards Stirling.

Now their route took them past the village of Kippen and the Castle of Arnprior, home of the Chief of the Buchanans. He, too, was entertaining several guests and, while he had plenty for them to drink, he was rather short of meat, so when he looked out of his window and saw a string of horses with fat deer over their backs he gave a great shout. 'Fetch that venison in here! My friends will have it for dinner.'

The hunters protested, 'But these are for King James!' Buchanan laughed. 'James may be King in Scotland, but I am King in Kippen!'

His men rushed out and surrounded the hunting party. They seized the venison and carried it into the castle.

It was a woebegone little band of hunters who arrived back at Stirling Castle and told the King what had happened. To their relief he did not blame them. He simply turned, went to his rooms and changed into his Gudeman's clothes. A short time later he was riding towards Arnprior.

When he reached the castle door he was confronted by a huge Highlander standing guard with an axe over his shoulder. Without waiting to hear what the stranger had to say, the Highlander told him that the Laird of Arnprior was at dinner and must not be disturbed.

'Is that so!' smiled James. 'Well, you go up and tell him that the Gudeman o' Ballengeich is come to feast wi' the King o' Kippen'.

Something in the stranger's air warned the sentry not to argue. He went up to the banqueting hall and delivered the message.

Silence fell over the party. The colour drained from Buchanan's face. He had heard of the King's adventures as the Gudeman and he suddenly realised just what he had done. Stealing from the King was a serious offence. Who knew what punishment might be meted out. Trembling, he went downstairs, knelt at James's feet and began a stammering apology.

The King said nothing and when, fearfully, Buchanan looked up into his face he was amazed to see that James was laughing.

'Rise up,' said James, 'and let us join the others.'

And so the King sat down as guest of honour at Buchanan's table and shared the dinner his host had stolen from him, and a right merry feast it was.

From that day, Buchanan got the nickname 'The King of Kippen' and he and the King of Scotland were the best of friends.

The Queen in the Tower

(1567-68)

Willie Douglas woke with a start. Something had wakened him, he did not know what. Could it have been oars on the water, a boat at the landing stage? He rose and went to the narrow window and peered out. It was still dark, though from the light in the sky, dawn was not far off. He could just make out the glimmering waters of the loch.

Next moment he heard the tramp of feet on the stone staircase. Along with the heavy tread of two or more men there was a lighter step. Who could they be at this hour? Not a word was spoken as they made their way to the Laird's apartments, then all was silence. Puzzled, Willie went back to bed, vowing to rise early in the morning to find out who had arrived in the night.

Willie's home was the island Castle of Loch Leven in Kinross-shire. Its ruins can still be seen today but at that time the building and its garden covered almost the entire island. Since then the level of the loch has been lowered, making the island bigger.

The castle was the home of Sir William Douglas, a rough red-bearded man and his wife, Lady Agnes. Also in the household was Sir William's mother, the formidable Lady Margaret. Sir William's younger brother George lived there too, though the two brothers had never hit it off and saw as little of each other as possible.

Lastly there was Willie, now 16. He was known as 'The Foundling' for he had been discovered as a baby drifting off the island in a small boat. Sir William had taken pity on the child and he and his wife had brought him up as if he was their own.

Still, it would not be surprising if Willie never felt wholly one of the family and perhaps he wondered now if there was something going on that he had not been told about.

Next morning he wasted no time in finding out whose footsteps he had heard in the night. What he learned fairly took his breath away. A prisoner had been brought to the castle and she was no less a person than Mary, Queen of Scots.

Willie had been only 10 when she had arrived in Edinburgh from France to claim the throne of Scotland. At first the people had greeted her with enthusiasm. She was young, high-spirited and attractive. She was not popular, though, with the leaders of the Reformed church. Mary was a Catholic and she made it clear that she had no intention of giving up her religion. This infuriated men like the preacher John Knox who also condemned her love of music and dancing.

As if to make herself even more unpopular, Mary married unwisely. The man she chose, Lord Darnley, was weak and undependable. When he died, suddenly, in a mysterious explosion in Edinburgh, the nobles at court, and reforming zealots like Knox, spread rumours that she had been involved in his murder.

They said that her friend, the Earl of Bothwell, had plotted it with her and even her own supporters turned against her when she married Bothwell soon after Darnley's death.

An army was raised to hunt down Bothwell, and his small force was defeated at Carberry Hill. Bothwell escaped and went abroad and Mary was taken prisoner and led back to Edinburgh where the streets were lined with screaming, jeering crowds.

Later, many of the people had relented towards her when they heard how she had been seen leaning from a window, crying for help. They remembered the beautiful smiling girl who had sailed into Leith and compared her with the pathetic figure, pale and unkempt, appealing for pity.

This shift of feeling towards Mary was one of the reasons her captors had decided to take her to Loch Leven. She could weep and scream as much as she liked there. No-one would hear or see her except her jailers.

From the first, Mary and Willie Douglas understood one another. Although she was sometimes ill for weeks at a time, she had a keen sense of humour which appealed to the young boy. When she felt well enough she would sing him the songs she had learned at the French court as a girl. She played the lute too and she enjoyed card-games, chess and billiards. On her good days, she made the stern island fortress a far brighter place than it had ever been.

There were dark times too though. There was the terrible day when she gave birth to still-born twins, after which she was ill for weeks. Around this time her enemies were trying to force her to sign papers renouncing the crown and passing it to her year-old son James whom she had hardly seen since his birth.

At last, the nobles grew so demanding that, in fear of her life, she gave in and signed the papers. It is said that one of her enemies, Lord Lindsay, held a knife to her throat and vowed to use it if she did not sign.

A few nights later, from her window, she saw blazing bonfires while the cannons outside the castle roared out across the loch. When she asked why, she was told it was to celebrate the crowning of her son. Now he was King of Scotland, though of course a regent was appointed to reign till he came of age.

Although Mary now had no powers, there was no sign of her captors giving her back her freedom. Perhaps they feared that if she was released she might gather a band of friends around her and seek revenge. And if she told how her abdication of the throne had been obtained by force, many would say it did not stand in law.

Mary realised that her only hope was to escape. She had two friends in the castle, Willie and his uncle George. They smuggled out letters for her, letters in which she appealed for help. She even wrote to her cousin, Queen Elizabeth of England, whom she had never met but who had once promised to come to her aid if Mary was ever in danger. Elizabeth ignored the call.

In the spring, George had a furious quarrel with his brother, the Laird, and was ordered off the island. This seemed like a blow to Mary's hopes of his helping her to escape, but in fact he went no further than Kinross on the shore of the loch. From there he redoubled his efforts to free Mary. Some people said he had fallen in love with her and this would not be surprising. She had great charm and may well have encouraged him so that he would do his utmost to get her off the island.

By this time other members of the castle household were feeling sympathy for her and believed that she should be set free. The servants had grown fond of her and they whispered amongst themselves that it was not right she should be held against her will like a criminal.

Sir William, however, had no intention of letting her go until the nobles in Edinburgh told him to do so. His mother, Lady Margaret, felt the same way and she made sure that Mary was almost constantly watched. If she did anything even slightly suspicious, news of it was instantly carried to Her Ladyship or to a soldier called Drysdale who was responsible for security on the island. He had been picked because he was an extreme Protestant and he took fierce delight in restricting Mary's movements.

Lady Margaret encouraged one of her daughters and a niece to spy on Mary and make sure that she was very seldom on her own. Even at night in her room they often kept watch on her while she slept.

All this made Mary even more determined to escape from the island. She had talked about it with George before he went to live in Kinross and he was now keeping in touch with young Willie through smuggled messages. Once George saw her from the shore as she walked in the garden. He rode on horseback as far as he could into the loch trying to signal to her. However, Drysdale and his guards saw what was going on and fired one of the cannons at him. Luckily the ball went over George's head but he very quickly retreated. Some years ago a cannon-ball was found in a spot in the loch which would have been in the line of fire, and it is thought to have been the one discharged that day.

On another occasion Willie accidentally dropped a letter he had been carrying secretly to Mary. One of the Douglas girls saw it fall and immediately ran to report him. He knew he would have to be much more careful after that.

At one time Willie and George thought of smuggling Mary off the island in a large wooden box. This idea was dropped as being too obvious—and most undignified for a Queen! Then one day George was sitting on the shore watching a coal-boat making its way across to the island. It regularly made the journey with coal for the fires and it was a sizeable vessel. This set George thinking of how he might seize the boat with a group of armed men and take the castle by storm. Somehow word of this plot reached Drysdale's ears and he alerted his guards to keep a close watch on all boats approaching the island.

Then Willie came up with an idea. A wall three metres high separated the castle from the shore where the island boats were moored. If Mary could clear that wall she could be rowed to the shore in no time. But could she do it? Willie discussed it with one of her servants who readily agreed to make the jump as an experiment. She got over the wall but badly damaged her ankle and so that was the end of Willie's idea.

Willie's next plan seemed less likely to fail. Mary was to be disguised as a laundry-woman and was simply to walk out through the castle gates and into a waiting boat. Mary put on the woman's clothes, hiding her face and head with a shawl. She walked past the guards and down to the boat, carrying her bundle. One of the boatmen was curious at the way she was hiding her face. He leaned over and tried to push the shawl aside. Mary pulled it back and in the quick movement he saw her long, slender fingers. These white hands were never those of a laundry-woman. He refused to take her in his boat, but to her relief he did not raise the alarm and she was able to return to the Castle without the Douglases knowing about the attempt.

George and Willie were still passing messages to one another but now George decided he must find a way of having a proper talk with him. He sent a letter to his mother, Lady Margaret, saying he was going abroad and asking permission to visit the castle to say goodbye. His mother was very sad at the news and persuaded Sir William to let him come.

At the first opportunity George saw Willie alone. The two were now of the same mind: the only way Mary was to escape was out through the Castle door. That meant stealing the key. It would be a risky business, but Willie said he would do it. To make sure of success, George was to arrange for a group of her supporters to be ready on the Kinross shore to meet Mary when she landed and escort her to safety. When George left the island he carried in his pocket one of the Queen's pearl ear-rings. This he was to send back to her as a signal that the rescue party was ready and waiting.

George and Willie had arranged a date for the attempt: 2 May. Two days before, Mary received a secret package. It was the ear-ring. She knew then that her friends awaited her arrival somewhere on the Kinross shore.

On the day set for her escape there was a May Day celebration including games in the courtyard. Willie was at the heart of the fun and the Queen joined him in a game of 'Follow My Leader'.

Afterwards, out of breath, she went to her room to rest and prepare herself for the adventure to come. As she lay on her bed she overheard her servants talking. She was alarmed to hear one of them say that there were a lot of mounted men over in the village. Worried lest they could be seen from the Castle, Mary hurried down to the garden to look across. To her dismay she was joined by Lady Margaret. As Mary tried to distract her attention in conversation, her Ladyship suddenly glanced across the water and caught sight of horsemen near the shore. Mary hastily changed the subject and led her back indoors. It was an anxious time for her, though. If Drysdale and his guards were to see the horsemen they might suspect something was afoot.

Sir William always came to Mary's room at suppertime, for she ate alone and before the rest of the household sat down to their supper in the dining-hall. As was his habit he wandered to the window and looked out. Mary's heart beat faster. He gave a great shout. Willie was down at the boats. Sir William bawled at him to leave them alone. Mary must have been close to panic. She knew what Willie was doing: he was fixing the chains on all the Castle boats but one, so that they could not be quickly cast off and pushed out into the water.

Mary distracted the Laird's attention by asking him to pour her a glass of wine. He did that and then went to have his own supper with the others.

Mary took a deep breath. The crucial time was drawing near. The two young Douglas girls came to see what she was doing, but she told them she was going to the room above to pray for a little. This was not unusual for she was very devout, and indeed it is probable that on this day she did go down on her knees and pray for deliverance.

One of her maids was involved in the escape plan and she now brought the Queen the clothes she was to wear on the journey. The girl was to accompany her so the two quickly got ready.

All depended now on Willie. Sir William sat at supper and the Castle keys lay on the table amidst the dishes and tankards. Willie brought him some wine and, as he set it down, he dropped his napkin over the keys. Next moment he had gathered them up and no-one had noticed. He nodded to one of the servants who slipped away to tell the Queen the moment had come. She and her maid made their way by the quietest corridors and flights of steps till they came to the postern gate where Willie awaited them. More than one servant saw them pass and, guessing what was happening, wished them well and stepped back.

Willie turned the great key in the lock. The door swung open and they were out. It was only a short way to the boat. Soon Willie was rowing towards the shore.

Some people say Willie threw the keys into the mouth of a cannon before they left the island. Others say he dropped them into the water as they crossed. A number of keys have been fished from the loch over the years and one of them may well have been the key to the postern gate.

It did not take long to row Mary to the shore. At once they were surrounded by her friends. George was there with a fine horse, fit for a Queen, ready saddled. He laughed as he told her he had stolen it from Sir William's own stables near Kinross. Mary swung on to its back and was off, George and Willie on either side and her other

51

friends behind. Some local people recognised the Queen and cheered and doffed their caps.

By now, in the Castle, there was consternation. Drysdale was livid with rage that his prisoner had tricked him. He stormed at his guards, blaming them, while the Laird had his head in his hands and was threatening suicide.

Drysdale and his men may well have been punished, but Lady Margaret and Sir William seem to have been forgiven by the nobles for their carelessness. They were even given another prisoner to guard, an Earl who was one of the Queen's supporters.

The escape party crossed the Forth by the ferry which was near where the Road-bridge stands now. More supporters joined them on the other side and they made for Niddry Castle in West Lothian where Mary slept as a free woman for the first time for many months. From there they moved on to Hamilton Palace. There she issued a proclamation stating that she was still Queen. Her abdication, she declared, did not stand since she had been forced to sign the papers.

The nobles would have none of it. They formed an army and confronted Mary's forces at Langside, near Glasgow. She watched the battle from the hill above. It was to be the turning-point in Mary's fortunes. Her supporters were defeated and fled in disarray. She found herself a fugitive. If at that moment she had crossed to France she would have been sure of a welcome and, who knows, she might one day have returned to Scotland and become Queen again. Instead, defying the advice of her closest friends, she made for England, believing that Queen Elizabeth would help her.

The truth was that Elizabeth distrusted and feared Mary. She saw her as a threat and she was jealous of Mary's charm and beauty. When she heard that Mary had crossed the Border she ordered that she be taken prisoner. Thus began Mary's 17 long years of captivity in England. During those years Elizabeth never went to see Mary though letters passed between them, most of them from Mary pleading for release.

Many plots to free Mary were hatched but none was successful.

Mary escapes from Loch Leven Castle

In the end she was beheaded at Fotheringay Castle in Northamptonshire in February, 1587.

Willie never deserted her. He remained in her service all his life, staying close to her and doing what he could to make her life bearable. He made at least one visit to France to seek help there and he tried at one point to stir up a rebellion against Elizabeth in the North of England.

George married twice with Mary's blessing, and became a prosperous citizen. He lived in the Borders and then at St Andrews.

You can see Loch Leven Castle on its island opposite Kinross and you can cross to it in a boat. It may be difficult to imagine what it looked like in Mary's time, but the views from it are not greatly changed from the way they were when Mary gazed out day after day during her months of imprisonment.

Bessie Bell and Mary Gray

(1646)

'Mary—are ye there?'

Mary went and threw up the window. 'Bessie?'

'Aye, it's me.'

Bessie scrambled into the room. She sat down on the edge of Mary's bed.

Outside Lynedoch House darkness was falling. In the candle-light Bessie's face was tense and pale. She had been running and her hair hung over her face like a gipsy's. Her dress was stained with mud. She didn't look like the young lady of Kinvaid House. Mary waited for her friend to get her breath back. She had little doubt what had brought Bessie. It would be more bad news about the Plague.

It was. 'There's mair fowk doon wi' it. Auld Graham, the shepherd. Mrs Thomson. Three o' the Stewart bairns.'

'Oh, Bessie, no!'

'Aye. But that's no' aa. I was speakin' tae Willie fae the Hillocks. He says there's a hail crood o' Perth fowk leavin' the toon and comin in tae the country. Ye ken whit that means.'

Mary did. They would bring the Plague with them and spread it far and wide as they had done in other rural districts.

Bessie buried her face in her hands. 'Whit are we tae dae, Mary?'

It did not take Mary long to decide. She had been thinking about it for days. She told Bessie her plan. When Bessie left Lynedoch House some time later there was a new light in her eyes. She hurried home to start preparations.

Next morning the two friends met at an arranged place, each carrying a bundle under her arm. They made their way through the woods to a hidden spot by a burn. There they cut branches and built themselves a bower or shelter. When it was finished they crept inside and sat together, laughing and joking as they used to do before the Plague came.

There were no houses in the vicinity, nobody ever came there. They would be able to live here safely until the epidemic was over.

Somebody, though, had to bring them food. Who was it to be? Bessie knew. 'James will dae it,' she said.

James was her boyfriend and she would have to let him know anyway where she was. She sent him a message and he came as quickly as he could, with a basket of provisions. Of course he and Bessie went for a walk in the woods as well before he left promising to return in two days time.

Life settled into a pattern for the two girls. By day they talked, played games and made improvements to their 'house'. Mary looked forward almost as much as Bessie to James's visits. It was good to hear news of their families and friends, though always sad when they heard of more deaths from the Plague.

'But dinna you worry,' James assured them. 'Ye're safe frae it here.'

One day, inside the basket of food was a small package.

'That's for you, Bessie,' said James.

'For me?' She opened it and held up a string of river pearls. 'Oh, they're bonnie. Look Mary!'

They were lovely, and when she hung them round her neck the pearls glowed against her brown skin.

She lay down to sleep that night holding the pearls in her hand. But during the night she awoke feeling weak and ill. She was worse in the morning and did not have the strength to leave the bower.

Mary nursed her friend, doing all she could to make her comfortable.

Then she, too, began to feel ill. With horror she recognised the signs.

The next time James came to see them it was all quiet in the dell by the stream. Inside the bower the two friends lay dead, clasped in each other's arms.

Bessie was still clutching the pearls James had brought her. It is to be hoped she never realised that it was his love gift that had killed them both. James had bought the necklace from a pedlar he had met near Perth. He was not to know the pedlar had stolen it from the neck of a Plague victim.

The two girls lie buried in a secluded spot near the river Almond. They were always together in their lives and they are not separated in death. Some say Bessie's sweetheart also died of the disease and lies at their feet. A stone slab was laid on the grave with these words on it:

'They lived, they loved, they died.'

A ballad was written about the tragedy:

Oh, Bessie Bell and Mary Gray,
They were twa bonnie lasses:
They biggit a bower on yon burn brae,
And theekit it o'er wi' rashes.

They theekit it o'er wi' rashes green,
They theekit it o'er wi' heather,
But the pest cam' frae the borrows toun
And slew them baith thegither.

They thocht to lie in Methven Kirk
Amang their noble kin,
But they maun lie on Lynedoch brae,
To beek fornent the sun.

Oh, Bessie Bell and Mary Gray,
They were twa bonnie lasses:
They biggit a bower on yon burn brae,
And theekit it o'er wi' rashes.

The 1646 Plague was one of a series of epidemics which swept through Scotland from the fourteenth century onwards for 300 years. Doctors of the time did not know what exactly the disease was and it is difficult for today's doctors to identify it for certain. They think it may have been bubonic plague, or possibly typhus.

Whatever it was, the Plague, or Black Death as it was often called, struck terror into the hearts of people in town and country. Today we can only imagine what it must have been like to see families and friends round about you dying off one by one.

Precautions were taken: ships sailing from infected ports were not allowed into harbour: traders such as the pedlar were not permitted to sell goods within the gates of towns: children were often kept indoors: heavy punishments were dealt out to people concealing a death within their home.

No doubt some of these precautions helped, but sadly, people failed to realise the real reason for the rapid spread of disease: the poor sanitation and dirty living conditions. They did not understand the connection between the disease and the open middens and polluted water and food. Not until standards were raised were people to be freed from the terror of the Plague.

Bessie Bell and Mary Gray were only two of many thousands of victims, but their sad deaths are still remembered in Perthshire over three centuries later.

Their simple grave lies hidden in a spot difficult to find, but perhaps that is how the two friends would have wished it.

The Great Montrose

(1650)

Scotland's glory, Britain's Pride,
As brave a subject as ere for monarch died,
Kingdoms in ruins often lie,
But great Montrose's acts will never die.

Pitcaple Castle, near Inverurie, nestles in the rolling Aberdeenshire countryside. One evening Lady Pitcaple looked out from one of the top windows and saw a cavalcade of horsemen approaching. As they drew closer she could see, in their midst, a stooped figure with one arm roughly bandaged across his chest. He was mounted on an aged and broken-down pony and his feet were tied together under its belly so that there was no chance of him escaping.

The horsemen rode up to the drawbridge and shouted that they wanted food and shelter for the night.

Lady Pitcaple dare not refuse. Her husband was away, fighting for the Royalists, and had taken the best of his men with him. The soldiers demanding entrance were anti-royalists, Commonwealth troops, but she was in no position to turn them away.

In any case she was curious about their prisoner. Although she could not see him properly there was something strangely familiar about his figure.

The horses clattered over the drawbridge and she stood in the doorway watching as the soldiers untied their captive and pulled him roughly from the pony's back. She saw him wince with pain, but he straightened his back as they pushed him towards the door. It was then she glimpsed his face and started back in dismay. It was her cousin, James Graham, Marquis of Montrose. Montrose, who, with a small army of fiery Highlanders had won battle after battle—Tippermuir, Inverlochy, Auldearn, Alford, Kilsyth.

It had seemed there was no stopping him or his Royalist cause. Then came Philiphaugh and terrible defeat. Montrose had been forced to escape to Norway. Later, to the joy of his supporters, he came back and gathered a fresh army.

It was soon clear there was to be no more glory. Instead, shipwreck off Orkney was followed by a rout at Carbisdale and then betrayal by a man he had trusted. Now, the Great Montrose was a prisoner. His army was scattered, the campaign was lost.

Lady Pitcaple gave no sign of recognition as he passed her in the doorway. Instead, she greeted the soldiers and told them there would be food, ale and beds for the night. Her servants led Montrose to a downstairs room and locked him in.

Soon, in the dining hall, there was a meal on the table and plenty of ale—the strongest there was in the cellars. The castle servants filled and refilled the tankards.

Lady Pitcaple slipped away to the room where Graham lay resting. First she took off the dirty bandage, washed his wound and put on a clean dressing. Then a servant brought him food and ale, though not as strong as the ale that was addling the brains of the troops upstairs. After he had eaten and drunk she told him he must sleep, but warned him not to sleep too soundly for she had a plan.

By 2 a.m. the castle was silent except for the snoring soldiers. Lady Pitcaple tiptoed to Montrose's room and told him to prepare for a journey. Outside, she said, a servant stood waiting with the finest horse from the stable.

'But how do I get outside,' he asked, 'without waking the soldiers?'

She smiled. 'I doubt if any of them will waken no matter how much noise you make. But you do not have to pass them. Look!'

She stepped to the wall of his room and pulled back a tapestry. Behind it was a secret door. She opened it and disclosed a narrow staircase. It led, she told him, to a secret tunnel. All he had to do was crawl along the tunnel and he would find himself outside the castle and on the other side of the moat. The horse would carry him to freedom.

Graham hesitated. He was thinking of what would happen to

Lady Pitcaple the next day when his escape was discovered. She would be arrested and imprisoned. The castle would be looted and probably burned. Her husband would be hunted down.

He pulled the door shut and drew back the tapestry. 'Sooner than go down that hole I will go to meet my accusers in Edinburgh.'

In the morning the troops continued on their way with their prisoner on the pony as before. When they got to Edinburgh, Montrose was put on trial and condemned to death.

A few days later, Lady Pitcaple went into the room he had used at the castle and found a robin perched on the bed. She knew what it meant. A local wise woman, the Guid Wife of Glack, had prophesied that when a robin appeared in the castle, it meant that a loved one was to die. It was no surprise to her when she heard that Montrose had been executed.

Not long afterwards, her husband returned home and after a short stay went off to fight again. Once more a robin appeared in one of the rooms and this time it was Lord Pitcaple who died, falling on the field of Worcester.

A robin has been seen on other occasions in the castle before a death, the last time in 1978 just before the death of the owner's cousin.

The Honours of Scotland

(1651—1881)

Like England, Scotland has her very own Crown Jewels. You can see them today in Edinburgh Castle, the gold Crown studded with precious stones, the elegant silver gilt Sceptre, and the richly decorated Sword of State. They are amongst the oldest Crown Jewels in all Europe and probably the most valuable objects in the whole of Scotland. Yet once they were carried in the bottom of a laundry basket and buried in the ground, and later forgotten about for over 100 years. This is how it happened...

The Honours of Scotland, as they are often called, were last used at the coronation of Charles II at Scone, Perthshire, in 1651. Later, when he fled to France and Cromwell attempted to spread his rule throughout Scotland, it was feared that his troops would seize the Crown Jewels and carry them south of the Border.

This was something the Scots people were not prepared to see happen. The Honours were part of their country's history and they had to be kept here. Realising that feelings were running high, the Edinburgh Parliament sent an urgent message to a man called William Keith. His family were Hereditary Keepers of the Crown Jewels so it was his duty, they told him, to remove them to a place of safety. The place they suggested was his own ancestral home, Dunnottar Castle, near Stonehaven, on the North-East coast.

Perched on a clifftop above the sea, Dunnottar was the perfect fortress. Any unwanted intruders could be easily repulsed. By the time Keith set off northwards with the Jewels, almost every other castle had fallen to the English. Only Dunnottar stood firm against them and its Governor, Captain George Ogilvie, was determined to do all he could to keep it out of English hands.

However, it had been easy enough for the Parliament in Edinburgh to order Keith to take the Crown Jewels to Dunnottar. It sounded simple enough, but first, he and his little party had to run the gauntlet of Cromwell's soldiers all the way there, and then, when they got within sight of Dunnottar, they found to their dismay that it was under seige. Cromwell's soldiers were guarding the entrance and carefully scrutinising every one who went in and out.

The party turned aside and made for the nearby Kinneff Manse where they explained their dilemma to the minister and his wife, Mr and Mrs Grainger. They talked well into the night.

Next morning, a laundry-woman approached the castle with a large basket of clean clothes on her shoulder. She exchanged smiles with the English soldiers as she passed between their lines. Once inside, she asked to be taken straight to the Governor.

You can imagine he was rather taken aback when the door opened and a laundry-woman was shown in. His surprise changed to amazement when she set down her basket, lifted the clothes out of it and showed him the Honours of Scotland hidden beneath. He laughed when he realised that the 'laundry-woman' was, in fact, Mrs Grainger, the minister's wife.

When she left she was given a pile of dirty linen which she carried through the enemy lines and home to Kinneff Manse. Perhaps the English soldiers thought she was smiling at them, but in reality she was smiling in satisfaction, for Ogilvie had promised that he would protect the Honours with his life.

Days passed and the English troops began to grow impatient. They were fed up of this cold, windswept camp and bored with keeping watch on the local people who went in and out of the castle. They began to suspect, too, that some of those going into Dunnottar were smuggling food and other provisions for the garrison. So one day they issued a stern warning, 'No more visitors of any kind.' No-one was to be allowed to enter or leave the castle. The very last person to be allowed out was a young girl cousin of the Governor's.

As she left, she told the English soldiers that she was going home because they feared the castle couldn't hold out very much longer. Food stocks were getting low and it was only a matter of time before the Governor would have to surrender.

This was true and of course the Governor knew that when Cromwell's men invaded the castle they would find the Crown Jewels. They would then be carried in triumph down to England. But he had promised Mrs Grainger that he would not allow this to happen, so he had devised a plan which his cousin now hurried to tell the Graingers at their Manse.

It was the custom for local women to gather seaweed on the rocky shore at the foot of the cliffs. In those days seaweed was cooked and eaten, and very good it was considered to be. A day or two later some of the women were there as usual at low tide, collecting the long strands and piling them into their baskets. One girl wandered a little further along than usual, until she was out of sight of the soldiers up on the cliff. Quickly she looked up at the castle and suddenly from out of the window snaked a long rope with a large bundle tied at the end of it. It came right down to where she was standing, she seized it, untied the bundle and put it into the basket, heaping seaweed over it. The rope was instantly pulled back up and she turned and made her way up the path to the clifftop.

A few minutes later she was in the minister's kitchen where she worked, for she was the Manse servant and had willingly agreed to take part in the ploy. She was a proud girl as she lifted the seaweed and showed Mr Grainger and his wife the bundle containing the Crown Jewels.

But what was to be done with them now? Word had reached the ears of Cromwell's officers that the Honours had been brought north and might be somewhere in the district. What a rich prize they would be! Cromwell would surely reward the man who found them and brought them to his feet.

Smuggling the Honours out of Dunnottar Castle

There was no time to be lost. Any day now a search might be made of local homes and there was no guarantee that the troops would respect the privacy of the Manse.

The Graingers hid the Honours where they thought no-one dare look—in their own bed—and then they waited for a moonless night. Fortunately they did not have to wait too long. When they were sure it was pitch black they crept out carrying the Royal Regalia wrapped in linen. Quickly they let themselves into the tiny church where, by the light of a candle, the minister prised up a paving-slab. The Crown and Sceptre were reverently laid in the hole beneath.

The Sword is said to have been too big to go into the space so it was concealed, in its case, in a dark corner of the church where it looked, at a glance, like part of the woodwork.

The Graingers had no idea how long the Honours might have to remain in their hiding-places. For all they knew it might be many years, long after they themselves had passed away. So that the secret would not die with them they wrote to William Keith's family telling them where they were hidden. Then they waited to see what would happen next.

As was feared, it was not long before the Governor of Dunnottar was forced to surrender and let Cromwell's men take possession. You can be sure that the soldiers searched the place from the turrets down to the dungeons seeking the missing Honours. They were furious that they did not find them, for they had been sure they were there.

Several years later, in 1660, came the Restoration. Cromwell's son, who had taken over from his father, was ousted and Charles II returned to England as King. As soon as she could, William Keith's wife went to London and told him the whereabouts of his Scottish Regalia.

It was a proud day for the folk of Kinneff when it was revealed that the Honours of Scotland had been concealed in the old kirk all that time. Now they were taken out and carried off to Edinburgh where they were brought out and put on display on any big State occasions.

Then in 1707 came the Union of the Scottish and English Parliaments. There seemed no longer a need for Scotland to have her own Royal Regalia. The precious items were put into a big chest or kist and put in store in Edinburgh Castle.

Time passed and everybody forgot where they were. It was over a century later, in 1818, that the great Scottish writer, Sir Walter Scott, decided that they must be rediscovered. He pressed for a search to be made.

It was remembered that there was a locked room in the castle and there was an old story that the Regalia had been deposited there. A special warrant was issued for permission to unlock the door and search the room.

The door was opened and the little party stepped into the dusty chamber. Before them on the floor sat a huge kist. There was no key to it so the King's Smith was sent for and ordered to force it open.

As he hammered at the lock, hearts sank. It sounded as if the chest was empty. The anxious spectators feared the worst as the lid was raised.

But it was not empty. At the foot lay bundles wrapped in linen. They lifted them up and, one by one, they unwrapped the Crown, the Sceptre, the Sword and other royal valuables. They were passed reverently from hand to hand as they gleamed in the light of day for the first time for over 100 years.

The news quickly spread through the castle. Soldiers of the garrison cheered, the Royal Standard was raised, and soon all Scotland was rejoicing.

Remember all this if you go to Edinburgh and look on the Crown Jewels. Today they are displayed in the Crown Room of the castle, the very chamber in which they lay hidden in a chest for so many years. The chest itself is there as well. Now visitors from all over the world file past these national treasures, not realising their amazing story and why they mean so much to every Scot.

Murder on Magus Moor

(1679)

It was a like a scene from a Western film. A group of armed men on horseback watched a carriage rumble across a bleak landscape. Then, at a signal from their leader, they set spur to their horses and galloped after it.

The coachman, seeing them coming, shouted a warning to the passengers inside and whipped up his horses. Shots were fired. The riders stormed level with the coach, forced it to a stop and wrenched open the doors.

It could have been happening in the lawless Wild West of America, but this was a moor near St Andrews in Fife.

Inside the coach that day were two passengers, Archbishop James Sharp and his young daughter, Isabel. The attack was not wholly unexpected. Sharp had been instructed by Charles II to impose an Episcopal form of worship on the Scottish people, and this he was only too keen to do. His methods had made him many enemies and the men waiting on the moor were among them. They were Covenanters, who believed in a Presbyterian church modelled on the ideas of a Frenchman called Calvin, a church without bishops or any kind of liturgy or show.

They believed that they had a special relationship with God and that this was impossible in the kind of worship conducted by Sharp and his priests.

Sharp was well aware that his life was always in danger. He had already been shot at in Edinburgh and he had set off for Fife knowing the journey was a risky one. There were a number of people in the area who hated his ideas and wished him dead.

However, it had gone very quietly. He and Isabel had spent a peaceful night with friends in Kennoway and now they were on the last lap. Only four miles lay between them and St Andrews. Magus

Moor, which they were now crossing, was a bleak place with little cover for an ambush. Already they could see St Andrews Bay ahead. They were breathing a little more easily, smiling and talking of what they would do in the Cathedral City.

Then came the shout from the driver. The coach lurched forward. A shot passed through the window, grazing the Archbishop's chest. Now men were riding alongside the horses, hacking at their harness with their swords. The coach shuddered to a stop.

One of the men pulled open the door and ordered the passengers out. Sharp sat back and refused. A sword swung at him, cutting him badly. As Isabel screamed, he clambered out and sank to his knees.

Isabel followed, pleading for her father's life. She and her father were aware of a man on a white horse who was taking no part in the attack but watched from a distance. Both turned to him, shouting for mercy.

He gave no reply but sat motionless as the others raised their swords and dealt the Archbishop a series of wild blows. He died in Isabel's arms and she cradled his head as they ransacked the coach and pocketed letters, money and other possessions.

It was not a quick hit-and-run affair. They took their time and it was the best part of an hour before they remounted their horses and galloped off, leaving Isabel weeping over her father's body. Three miles away they stopped to give thanks to their God for giving them the chance to rid the world of their enemy.

When Isabel reached St Andrews with her father's corpse there was widespread horror. Even many Covenanters were disgusted at the brutality of the crime. Charles II was furious. He demanded that the killers be hunted down and punished. The Privy Council in Scotland were just as enraged. One of those caught and hanged was the man who had sat on the white horse and played no part in the murder. His name was Hackston of Rathillet and it was enough for the Council that he had been there and had not tried to save Sharp's life. His body was dismembered and his hands are said to be buried in the old kirkyard in Cupar.

The murder on Magus Moor deepened the bitterness between

the Covenanters and those in Scotland who wanted an Episcopal form of worship. It led to what became known as the Killing Times, when there was bloodshed and misery on a terrible scale.

As for Isabel Sharp, she could never forget her father's death and that hour of terror but she married happily, becoming Mrs Cunningham of Barns, in Fife.

It is said that a coach and horses can sometimes be heard on the road above St Andrews, rumbling through the night, carrying Archbishop James Sharp to his terrible death.

A cairn near Pitscottie marks the spot where the murder took place. Fife Folk Museum has items relating to the event, including a boot that was worn by Hackston who watched from his white horse.

Rob Roy, Adventurer

(1691)

The huge herd of cattle moved slowly along the drove road. They were small black beasts, docile enough, only needing a tap now and then from the men tramping alongside, sticks in their hands. The men were Livingstones and they were driving the cattle to the great market at Stirling.

Ahead lay Flanders Moss, a wide marsh of which many tales were told. Lose yourself in it, it was said, and you would never be seen again. The drovers would skirt it, keeping to the dry ground, and passing through the villages of Kippen and Buchlyvie. Going that way they would be safe from danger.

In fact, another kind of danger awaited them. The countryside round Buchlyvie was swarming with Highlanders and their leader was going from one group to the other with his orders.

He was Rob Roy MacGregor and he guessed that the Livingstones would come this way. They were no friends of his and he had decided to add their cattle to his own herd in the Trossachs.

He looked, at first sight, an unlikely leader. His legs were short and most of his men towered above him but he made up for his lack of height with unusually long arms. They had great strength in them and when he had a sword in his hands he was a formidable opponent.

He knew all about the Livingstones and their herd and he expected them to reach Buchlyvie that morning. There he would ambush them and drive away the cattle.

While some of his men kept watch for the approach of the herd others hung about in the village. The hours passed and there was no sign of the Livingstones. At first the villagers had been too frightened to object to the wild strangers in their midst, but as the day wore on they grew bolder. They sent word of what was happening to the neighbouring villages of Kippen and Balfron and appealed for help to drive the Highlanders out. They were fearful of a skirmish taking place between the MacGregors and the Livingstones, right on their doorstep. They were also afraid lest the Highlanders turn to looting local homes before they left.

Some of the braver men armed themselves with sticks and farm implements and gathered in a threatening crowd. When Rob Roy heard of this he thought it better to avoid trouble. He led his men away from the village to moorland near Kippen. This no doubt was a relief to the folk of Buchlyvie but raised anger and dismay in Kippen.

Out from the village came a crowd brandishing clubs and sickles. At the same time there came into view what the MacGregors had been waiting for: the Livingstones and their cattle.

Rob first had to deal with the villagers. He had no quarrel with them and no doubt understood their feelings. As they advanced on his men brandishing their rough weapons he ordered the MacGregors to fight them off with the flats of their broadswords so that none of them would be badly injured.

The local men were no match for Rob's skilled swordsmen. They fell back in disarray and as soon as they did the MacGregors turned and swooped on the Livingstones. This time there was no mercy and the swords were used in earnest.

Soon Rob Roy was leading his men homewards with the Livingstone herd. To punish the locals for the trouble they had given him he rounded up many of their cattle as well.

It was through this exploit that Rob Roy's name first became widely known.

His early life was a balance between lawful activities and cattle-stealing expeditions like this one. There is no saying which side of his nature would have won, but the matter was decided for him. He had borrowed a large sum of money for the purchase of cattle and entrusted a drover called MacDonald to go and collect them. MacDonald disappeared with the money.

That was the turning point. Rob's wife and children were evicted from their home and Rob Roy became an outlaw famed for his daring exploits.

He had many adventures. Once he was captured through trickery and placed on horseback. The little procession of riders approached the Fords of Frew, a crossing over the Forth. It was night and the waters were swollen and icy cold. Another man sat on horseback with Rob Roy and the two were tied together with rope so that the outlaw could not escape.

Unknown to his captors he was carrying a small knife. Now he cut through the rope and threw himself from the saddle into the water. At once he slipped out of his plaid. As it floated away his captors shot at it and struck it with their swords while Rob Roy swam to the safety of the bank.

In his later years he mellowed and settled down to live a quiet life in Balquhidder in Perthshire. He died in bed there after calling on a piper to play the lament 'I Shall Return No More'. He lies in the little graveyard with other members of his family.

The Rob Roy and Trossachs Centre at Callander celebrates his adventures and there is a cave where he is said to have hidden near Inversnaid, Loch Lomond. There is a fine statue of him (showing his short legs and long arms!) at Stirling and another above a burn at Peterculter, Aberdeenshire.

Sir Walter Scott's novel *Rob Roy* helped to spread his fame and though it is by no means a true account, Scott was able to draw on stories about the outlaw that were still going the rounds in the Scotland of his day.

Other books about his life have been published in more recent times and it is not surprising that a film version of his adventures was a great success when released a few years ago.

The Glen of Weeping
(1692)

Towards the close of the seventeenth century many in the West Highlands were feeling resentful and rebellious. The reason: the Catholic James VII had been driven into exile and his place on the English throne taken by William of Orange, a Protestant Dutchman and no friend to the Catholics and Episcopalians of the Scottish Highlands. Most of the Highlanders wanted nothing to do with him: they longed instead for James's return from France.

William knew of their dislike for him, but Scots politicians in Edinburgh had gone along with their counterparts in England in accepting him so he had no sympathy for anyone who did not accept his right to rule the two countries.

The King could have tried to win the waverers over by showing them he could be trusted not to interfere with them and their ways of worship. That, however, was not his style. He was an impatient man and he wanted them to fall into line now, not later.

His closest ministers agreed and, to be fair to William, there were Scots politicians, Lowlanders many of them, only too keen to take a harsh line with the Highlanders. The plan that was worked out seems to have been more their work than William's.

This was what it was: on 17 August a message was sent out to all clan chiefs telling them that by the end of the year they must swear loyalty to the new King. Any chief who failed to do this would be punished. They had till the first of January 1692 to comply.

In Glen Coe, old Alasdair MacDonald received the message and laid it aside. James was the only monarch he recognised, not this foreign usurper. He had been heartbroken when word had reached him of James's defeat at the Battle of the Boyne in Ireland and he still hoped for James's return from exile. Well, no doubt James would learn of this order to his subjects and send word advising what they should do. MacDonald decided to wait until he heard his King's wishes.

Most of the other chiefs were of the same mind. On their behalf two messengers had been sent on a secret mission to France to ask James for his advice. They would all wait until the two returned. There was plenty of time...

Weeks passed and the messengers had still not returned from France. October...November. Still no word. The truth was that James could not make up his mind what to tell them. He never had been good at coming to decisions.

While he dithered, others were rubbing their hands. One of them was John Dalrymple, whom William had made his Lord Advocate and Secretary of State. Dalrymple had switched sides from James to William to further his ambitions. Utterly ruthless, he was prepared to do anything that would advance his career. Also, as a Borders man, he held only contempt for Highlanders with their uncouth ways. He would gladly teach them a lesson, especially if it won him more favours from King William.

In his rooms in Kensington Palace, London, Dalrymple watched the days and weeks slip past with ill-concealed glee. If some of the chiefs were to fail to meet the deadline, he would take the greatest pleasure in punishing them in King William's name. In the meantime he wrote to friends in power in Scotland, alerting them that tough action was going to be required. In one of his letters, dated 3 December, he said they might need to take 'a severe course' with the MacDonalds of Glen Coe. He suggested that, now winter had come on, it was 'the proper season to maul them in the long cold nights'.

Still old MacDonald and the other chiefs were waiting for word from France. At last, on 12 December, the swithering James made up his mind. He signed an order telling them they had best swear loyalty to William.

There were now only 19 days to go before the deadline. Every minute mattered. One of the messengers, Duncan Menzies, left Paris at once carrying the vital order. It took him nine days to get to Scotland and he arrived exhausted after the long and arduous journey. But he wasted no time. Soon, from his home near Dunkeld, a fleet of messengers was heading out to various corners of the Highlands to inform the clans of the ex-King's decision. As quickly as word was reaching them the chiefs were setting out to do as James advised. This meant travelling to the nearest town to find a Sheriff who could accept the oath of allegiance on William's behalf. It would then be conveyed to Edinburgh to be officially recorded.

MacDonald did not get his message until 28 or 29 December. It could not have come at a worse moment: heavy snow had fallen and some hill tracks were blocked and others difficult. Nevertheless he set off for Fort William, riding on a mountain garron and followed by several servants.

The little party reached Fort William late on the 29th and MacDonald asked to see the officer commanding the garrison, Colonel Hill. When he explained he had come to swear his loyalty, Hill stared at him in amazement. Did MacDonald not realise he had to see the Sheriff of Argyll who was in Inveraray many miles away? This was a bitter blow for the old chief. It meant that he had to retrace his steps, for Inveraray was the other side of Glen Coe. To make things worse he learned that the quickest route was blocked with snow and that he would have to go the longest way, by Loch Linnhe.

Time, he knew, was running desperately short if he was to swear allegiance to William before the deadline. By this time he fully realised the dangers of being late. Not just he but his entire clan of MacDonalds would be at the mercy of the authorities. There was no saying what they might do—with all the strength of the law behind them.

Although exhausted and worn out, he rode off at once into the driving snow.

With his followers he crossed the ferry at Ballachulish and took the shore road by Loch Linnhe. It was a hard journey for an old man in terrible conditions, but they were more than half way there when, just after they had reached Loch Creran, suddenly, barring the track in front of them was a platoon of Government redcoats.

Their leader demanded to know who they were and where they were going. MacDonald explained and showed him a letter of introduction that Colonel Hill had given him. The man was not satisfied. He insisted on taking the little party to nearby Barcaldine Castle where the army had set up a temporary headquarters. There the old man had to explain his story all over again.

The captain in charge was suspicious. He refused to let MacDonald go on. For 24 hours he and his retainers were held prisoner—precious time that was to cost his clansfolk dear.

It was early on the first of January when MacDonald and his servants were at last allowed to leave. They pressed on as quickly as they could, stopping when darkness fell to spend the night in a sheiling above their destination, Inveraray.

In the morning they rode into the town and sought the Sheriff of Argyll, Sir Colin Campbell.

Alas, he was not there. He had been spending Hogmanay with friends and his return had been delayed by the stormy weather. In near despair, MacDonald took rooms at an inn to await Campbell's return.

It was 5 January before he came back. MacDonald was early on his doorstep. He found Campbell in a bad mood. He was still furious at having been storm-bound. He greeted the old man angrily. Did he not realise that the date for swearing loyalty was past? Like all the other chiefs he had been given over four months' warning: why had he left it till now? MacDonald was a proud man, but now, perhaps for the first time in his life, he was reduced to pleading. He told Campbell about the weather, the redcoats, his mistake in going to Fort William at the start of his journey. There were tears in his eyes as he humbled himself before Sir Colin.

At last Campbell relented. 'Very well,' he said grudgingly. 'Come back tomorrow and I will accept your oath.' MacDonald's relief was enormous. His clanspeople should now be safe from punishment. Of course word had still to be sent to Edinburgh but he had Campbell's promise that he was accepting the oath.

Next day he and his party were in cheerful mood as they mounted their garrons and headed for home. As if to help them on their way, a thaw had set in and the snows were melting so they made good speed back to Glen Coe. There his people gathered round him. He had been away longer than they expected and they had grown anxious. There was much smiling and nodding when he told them they had nothing to worry about. He had sworn the loyalty of his clan to the new monarch and it had been accepted. They could get on with their lives in peace.

And so they did, for a brief time. They were not too worried when, early in February, they heard that a company of around 120 troops had been sighted heading towards Glen Coe. The soldiers halted at the mouth of the Glen and MacDonald sent his son John to meet them. John found that they belonged to the Earl of Argyll's Regiment, recruited from Clan Campbell and commanded by Captain Robert Campbell of Glenlyon.

Now the Campbells and MacDonalds had had their differences in the past. Clan feuds were common in these days. The MacDonalds were as fiery as anybody else. But Captain Campbell was a relative of old MacDonald's. What is more he bore a letter from his Colonel politely asking MacDonald if he would provide the soldiers with board and lodgings for a few days. In the Highlands hospitality was never refused. The area is still famous for it today. John led them into the Glen and took them to his father who at once agreed to his request.

The homes of the MacDonalds were scattered all over the Glen. It took some time to find beds for all the soldiers, one or two in this house, three in that one. At last everyone was accommodated and the MacDonald families started to make friends with their unexpected guests.

Conditions inside the houses were very cramped and uncomfortable, for in those days animals such as cows and horses often lived under the same roof as their owners, especially in winter. But once they were fixed up the Campbells were no trouble. During the day they would be out drilling and exercising and in the evenings they joined their hosts round the fire to exchange stories and songs. No doubt there was pipe music as well.

On the evening of 12 February a runner came up the Glen and handed Captain Campbell a message. Then a new officer rode in, a Captain Drummond. He drew Campbell aside and they had a long talk. Campbell then told John MacDonald that he and his troops would be leaving Glen Coe quite soon and went to speak to his officers. Soon a message was being passed amongst the soldiers, from mouth to mouth, house to house all down the Glen.

Everybody went to bed, MacDonalds and Campbells alike. Glen Coe lay silent. The hours passed. Then, between 4 and 5 in the morning the Campbells arose, dressed and armed themselves. They slipped from the houses and gathered at a mustering point. Those MacDonalds who heard them moving about thought they were preparing to leave the Glen. They turned over and went to sleep again.

At 5 a.m. there was a knock at old MacDonald's door. An officer stood there and behind him a group of soldiers. The officer called to MacDonald that he had come to say goodbye and to thank him for his hospitality over the past days.

MacDonald and his wife dressed hastily, but they were barely ready when the door burst open and several musket shots rang out. MacDonald died instantly. His wife, wounded and almost naked, fled to the hills. The two servants lay dead by their master's side.

All over the Glen similar scenes were taking place. The MacDonalds, who had given the soldiers food and drink, who had shared their company, were being dragged from their homes and shot down. Young and old, men, women and children—it made no difference. Their screams for mercy were ignored as the brutal slaughter raged.

In all nearly 40 met their deaths in this way, but many more were to die of cold and exposure on the bleak snow-covered hills to which they ran for safety.

It is said even more would have been shot, but that some of the soldiers could not bring themselves to carry out the task. Remembering the MacDonalds' kindness to them they let them escape into the corries.

The soldier spares a mother and child

When Drummond and Campbell found that many of the MacDonalds had gone into hiding in the hills they commanded the troops to go after them and hunt them down. Some did but others did not. One young woman was sheltering in a hollow with her baby. An officer heard her singing to the child to soothe it. He sent a soldier to despatch them both with his sword. The soldier went, but could not bring himself to do it. There was a dog by the girl's side—he killed it and returned, showing the bloodstained sword to the officer as 'proof' that he had done what he was told.

When it was all over, the Glen was deserted. Only the corpses remained in the smoking ruins of the houses, for most of them had been set on fire. Their thatched roofs caught light easily and many still glowed red in the grisly light of dawn.

So why had it happened? Who was to blame? King William himself had signed the order, though for him it was just another paper to sign. Perhaps he failed to realise what it was to lead to.

John Dalrymple got most of the blame and certainly, as we have seen, he had urged that action be taken. He wanted an example to be made of the MacDonalds so that other clans would know what to expect if they did not toe the line in future.

There was such strong feeling against him that eventually he had to give up his post as Secretary of State. His career in politics was blighted but it did not prevent him gaining fresh honours from the King, on whom he continued to fawn.

The blame was not all his though. Several Army officers were responsible for passing on the orders without questioning them, and Captain Robert Campbell was surely the most guilty of all. He had been in command of the soldiers who had carried out the massacre at his direct orders.

When news leaked out of what had happened in Glen Coe, there was widespread horror, not just in Scotland but in England too. An enquiry was set up but it did not dig very deep. No-one was really punished for what had happened.

As for the MacDonalds who survived that night, many were given shelter by other clans. In time most of them returned to the

Glen to rebuild their houses and pick up the pieces of their shattered lives.

The massacre has never been forgotten. Glen Coe is often called 'The Glen of Weeping', and although it happened a long time ago, there is still a sadness clings to its mountain slopes. Close your eyes in some of its quiet corners and you may think you hear the cries of children, the screams of women and the terrible sound of musket fire.

Hang Captain Porteous!

(1736)

Captain Porteous swaggered down Edinburgh's High Street. He always walked like that wherever he went and if you didn't get out of his way quickly enough he would give you a cuff to remind you the next time.

People knew better than to argue with him. As Captain of the City Guard he could have you flung in the Tolbooth and once in there it wasn't so easy to get out again.

He was a bully was Captain Porteous, and the worst of it was, he had power and authority on his side. But... 'He'll go too far one day,' people muttered darkly—and he did.

It all began when the Guard arrested two men for stealing goods from a customs house. Robertson and Wilson were thieves, there was no doubt about that. In fact they were smugglers. They stole and sold goods imported from abroad which should have had excise duty charged on them. These charges were resented by many Edinburgh folk so there was quite a lot of sympathy for the two amongst their fellow citizens and the resentment turned to anger when it was learned that they had been sentenced to death.

It was the talk of the howffs (bars) as the day drew near when the executions would take place.

At that time prisoners awaiting the death sentence were led out from gaol every Sunday to attend the service in the nearby Tolbooth Church. This, it was hoped, would help them to repent of their sins and die in the right frame of mind.

The interest in the Robertson and Wilson case meant that members of the congregation already in their seats craned to watch the two prisoners being led in to the pew reserved for them at the front of the church. Four soldiers sat beside them as they waited for the service to begin.

The doors stood open, for people were still coming in, and perhaps it was the sight of the open door, but suddenly Robertson leaped up, vaulted the pew and dashed out of the church. No-one tried to stop him and the soldiers were delayed by Wilson who had risen to his feet and was struggling to get free and follow him.

It was said afterwards that he knew he could not escape but was simply creating a delaying tactic so that his friend would win freedom. It worked, for by the time two of the guards rushed outside, Robertson had vanished.

In the hours and days that followed the city was searched from end to end without success. Porteous, of course, was furious. It was bad for his reputation to have let a criminal escape justice. He had seen people laughing at him when they passed in the street. That made his blood boil. Well, at least he still had Wilson. He looked forward with relish to watching him swing from the gibbet in the Grassmarket.

He shared none of the worries of the Provost and Magistrates who sensed the hostility of ordinary folk to the carrying out of the sentence. Why, they said, should Wilson suffer the death penalty when his friend had got off with it Scot free? That's what folk were asking and it was being said that while Robertson was a real bad egg, the unfortunate Wilson was quite a decent chap. Look how, unselfishly, he helped his friend to escape...

To ensure there was no crowd trouble on the day of the execution, the Magistrates arranged for four companies of soldiers to be drawn up in the Lawnmarket which the prisoner would pass along on his way from theTolbooth.

Porteous being the type of man he was, the sight of the soldiers infuriated him. He took their presence as an insult to him and his Town Guard. As if he and his men could not handle this on their own! The procession made its way to the Grassmarket with Porteous well to the fore. Hangings then were a public spectacle and a crowd always gathered to watch. This time there were even more people than usual, with folk leaning from their windows in the high buildings along the route. The Grassmarket was thronged.

Porteous was enjoying himself. He was in charge and that was how he liked it. The orders were given to the hangman and Wilson climbed the steps, a pathetic figure. The crowd watched in silence as the noose was placed around his neck. He gave a last look heavenwards and then next moment his body was jerking and turning on the end of the rope.

A murmur rose from the onlookers. Their eyes turned to the hangman.

He was a deeply unpopular figure. People despised him for the unsavoury job he did and quite often a stone or two would be flung in his direction just to let him know what they thought of him. It was the same this time. A stone, a lump of dirt, flew through the air. It was no worse than usual and if Porteous had ignored the missiles, and marched his men off, that would have been the end of it.

But, still smarting with indignation at the presence of the soldiers in the Lawnmarket, he was desperate to show his authority. Turning to the ranks of the City Guard he shouted to them to fire. The men, amazed, were hesitant. Some half-raised their muskets, others stared at Porteous in disbelief. His face now purple with rage, he yelled at them and brandished his arm at the crowd. The men had no choice—they fired. Most of them, though, aimed their muskets upwards, hoping not to hit anyone. Their shots went high, above the heads of the crowd, but they forgot about the spectators at their windows. There were screams as several of them were struck.

There were cries from below, too, and then followed several moments of sheer panic as the crowd rushed for cover to neighbouring wynds and closes. Behind them dead and wounded littered the ground.

Around 30 people died on the spot or later from their wounds including one of those who had been watching from a window. As the news spread like wildfire through the city there was universal anger at what had happened.

The Provost and Magistrates had to act. They ordered the arrest of Porteous. Thus the bold Captain found himself in a cell in the

Tolbooth into which he had thrown so many people. Now he was the prisoner, not the jailer.

He was tried in court on a charge of 'wilful murder' and sentenced to die on the very same spot as the one on which Wilson had met his death. The hanging was set for 8 September.

But Porteous was determined to cheat the gallows. He sent a petition for mercy to Queen Caroline. Day after day he looked for a response and none came. Now it was the 8th. The streets were packed to suffocation. Everyone was eager to see him go to his death.

The appointed time came and went. The crowds grew restless. Rumours were spreading from mouth to mouth. It was said that he had got off, that he was not to be hanged after all. At last the Magistrates made an announcement. A reply from the Queen had arrived. Porteous had been granted a reprieve. The hanging was postponed for six weeks.

When the news spread amongst the crowd there was fury. Outside the Tolbooth, the mob grew larger every minute. Suddenly the sound of splintering wood rang out. Several men had broken down the door and rushed inside. But where was Porteous? They found him trying to escape up the chimney.

He was dragged outside and carried through the crowded streets. They stopped only once, outside a ropemaker's. The door was burst open and a length of rope seized, then they continued their triumphant march to the Grassmarket.

In vain Porteous pleaded and cried for mercy. Nothing was going to stop the mob now. They needed no hangman but did the job themselves. The hated Captain of the Guard would bully no-one ever again.

When word of the riot reached London, the Prime Minister, Robert Walpole, took a very serious view. Rewards were offered for the names of the ringleaders but no names were forthcoming. For a time it was thought that Edinburgh would be subjected to some form of heavy punishment. In the end it was the Provost who got the blame. He was dismissed from his post and a fine was levied on the city and paid over to John Porteous's widow.

As for Robertson, who had made his escape from the church, he found his way to safety in Holland, where it is said he settled down happily far from the scenes of probably the worst riot Edinburgh has ever seen.

Flora and the Prince

(1746)

When Charles Edward Stuart, the 'Bonnie Prince', galloped off the field after the disastrous Battle of Culloden on 16 April, he did not think for a moment that it marked the end of his hopes of becoming King of Scotland and England.

He was to spend the next five months on the run trying to get out of this country and over to France. Once there he intended to set about immediately planning another Uprising, a fresh invasion of Scotland.

It was this ambition that kept his spirits high as a small band of loyal friends, some Scots, others Irish, smuggled him from one hiding-place to another, protecting him from discovery. He slept in huts, bothies and caves, and some nights he had no shelter at all except the rocks and the heather. There were sea crossings in open boats and rough treks over wild country often at dead of night and in rain and wind. (Highland summers were no different then!)

Throughout the whole ordeal he never seems to have wavered in thinking of himself as the future King of this country. The people he met along the way shared his hopes and dreams and most of them treated him as if he was already their King.

One of the few people not over-awed by Prince Charles was Flora MacDonald. She respected him, she helped him, but she did it on her own terms and in her own way.

She was 24 at the time, a good-looking young woman with large, dark eyes and a firm chin that told of her determined character. She had been brought up on the island of South Uist in the Outer Hebrides, but her father had died and her mother was now re-married and living in Skye. Flora spent her time between Skye and South Uist where her brother still lived in the family home.

It was fortunate for Charles that she happened to be on Uist when he was in one of the tightest corners of his five months on the run.

With his small group of protectors he had spent several weeks lying low on and around the island. Now he had just two compan-ions, Neil MacEachain and Felix O'Neil. Both had served under the French flag so were trained soldiers, resourceful and fit. Neil had been born in South Uist and as a youth had studied for the priesthood in Paris. He spoke Gaelic, English and French. Felix was more Spanish than Irish, though he had risen to Captain in an Irish regiment.

These two were well aware of the danger the Prince was in. The Government had offered an astonishing £30,000 for information leading to his capture. Such a sum, in those days, would have made any Highlander rich beyond his wildest dreams. His protectors were not to know that, of all the people who encountered him on his wanderings, none made any attempt to earn the reward. Two Pres-byterian ministers, father and son, are the only people known to have tried to win the money.

What Neil and Felix did know now was that the authorities had a pretty good idea that the Prince was on Uist and had sent troops in to search for him while their ships patrolled the coasts.

They were, of course, looking not just for Charles but for any of the hundreds of Jacobite fugitives who had been on the run since Culloden. Outlaws in their own country, they were being hunted down throughout the Highlands and either shot or herded into prisons. Many were put to death while others were sent into exile in foreign lands.

The greatest prize the searchers sought was Bonnie Prince Charlie himself and the rumour that he was on South Uist was the signal for troops to be poured onto the island and its neighbour, Benbecula.

The safest place Neil and Felix found on Uist was a bothy in the remote glen of Corradale tucked deep in a hollow in the hills. The three lingered there for several days undisturbed. Charles joined them in fishing and killing birds for food and they talked and entertained one another well into the night.

But as more troops descended on Uist, it was clear the net was closing in. Sooner or later a detachment of soldiers would find their way to Corradale. There had already been one near thing when, on a quick dash from the island of Wiay to South Uist in the dark they had been almost rammed by two patrolling vessels. Scrambling ashore, the party lay low for the rest of the night in a rocky cavern. In the morning when they looked out, one of the boats was still lying off the coast so they had to spend the rest of the day and another night in the narrow cave until the boat moved away.

Next time they might not be so lucky.

Where could they go to elude capture? Neil and Felix scratched their heads and decided on Skye. There were Jacobites there who would help them and it was a mountainous island riddled with places of concealment. It would also be just as convenient for a French ship calling in to take Charles back to France—providing it could run the gauntlet of the patrol vessels.

The two soldiers knew the journey to Skye would be risky. They might easily run into militia men on their way to the boat or when they reached Skye. On the voyage they might be stopped by a boarding party.

Then one of them hit on an idea. What if Charles was in disguise—female disguise? They put the suggestion to him a little anxiously, but to their delight he agreed eagerly and seemed highly amused at the thought of it.

However, a woman travelling alone with a group of men might be an object of suspicion. If, though, she was a servant accompanying her mistress, no-one would take any notice of her.

'Flora MacDonald!' exclaimed Neil. He knew her and remembered how she often went to Skye to visit her mother. It would be quite natural for her to take a servant girl along with her. She was also well connected and had friends in some of the best families in the islands. She would surely not be suspected of assisting an outlaw. The question was, would she do it? Although it was night-time, they set out with Charles to go and see her. First they called at her brother's house at Milton, where they learned that Flora was spending the night in a summer sheiling or cottage on the hill above. They made their way up the hill.

Charles waited nearby in the shadows while his friends went in and put their plan to her.

Some writers like to give the impression that she agreed at once, but she herself wrote later that she had raised 'many qualms and objections'. The idea was, she thought, 'fantastical and dangerous'.

Only when the Prince was called out of the dark and she had questioned them all closely did she consent. She told them that she would enlist the aid of a friend, Lady Clanranald, who lived at Nunton on the neighbouring island of Benbecula. If Charles could be taken there to be dressed for the journey they could sail to Skye from nearby Rossinish.

Flora said she could do even more than that. Her stepfather was a Captain in the Government forces. Because of the hunt for Charles he and his men had been sent to Benbecula to join in the search. He was, however, just as much a Jacobite as his step-daughter and had no intention of capturing his Prince.

There was one way in which he could be specially useful. Since the Rising had been crushed at Culloden, the Highlands and Islands had been under martial law. One of the rules imposed by the Government was that anyone travelling from one place to another was required to carry a pass. Without one, any Highlander was liable to arrested. Flora was sure that her stepfather would supply a pass for her 'maid'.

And so he did. They decided to give Charles the name Betty Burke, and along with passes for her and Flora, her stepfather wrote this letter to his wife Marion which Flora could take with her and show to anyone who questioned her on the trip:

91

My Dear Marion,

I have sent your daughter from this country, lest she should be in any way frightened with the troops lying here. She has got one Betty Burke, an Irish girl, who, as she tells me, is a good spinster. If her spinning pleases you, you may keep her till she spins all her lint: or if you have any wool to spin you may employ her. I have sent Neil MacEachain along with your daughter and Betty Burke to take care of them.

I am your dutiful husband,

Hugh MacDonald.

It is thought that the reason they decided to make Betty an Irish girl was that if anyone were to overhear Charles speaking they would take his Continental accent for an Irish one!

Charles and Flora now said goodbye to each other until all was ready for them to sail. Charles and his two friends had to find cover before daybreak. They made for the secret glen of Corradale where they had hidden before, but as dawn broke they were still three miles from it on the slopes of Hekla. They dared not travel further, but went to ground behind a rock and settled down to spend the daylight hours there.

Charles, however, was impatient to hear how Flora was getting on with the arrangements. So much depended on her persuading Lady Clanranald to help. He insisted that Neil MacEachain go to Nunton on Benbecula, to find out if Flora was at Lady Clanranald's. Neil got as far as the ford between South Uist and Benbecula and there he was arrested and held overnight. However, he managed to spin the soldiers a story and they set him free in the morning to continue his journey.

The same thing had happened to Flora. She had been allowed across the ford but had been stopped on the Benbecula side by militia men demanding to see her pass. Talking to them she found that they were from Skye and were under the command of her stepfather. 'Send for him,' she told them. 'He will vouch for me.' They were not convinced, and locked her up under armed guard.

The Prince disguised as Betty Burke

However, they did send word to her stepfather and he arrived in the morning and immediately ordered her release and took her to breakfast. They were still at breakfast when a group of soldiers appeared with another prisoner—Neil MacEachain.

The soldiers were all told to go and then, in privacy, the three put their heads together. Flora was to proceed to Lady Clanranald's at Nunton. From there she hoped to go that very afternoon with food and clothes to Rossinish. Neil must make his way back to Hekla and bring the Prince to Rossinish as quickly as possible. There was a cottage there they could use before setting sail for Skye.

This time Neil was not delayed on his journey but made good time back to Hekla where the Prince and Felix sprang up from behind the sheltering rock to hear the news.

The three waited till darkness fell before they began their journey. Somehow they had to get over the narrow channel between South Uist and Benbecula. The usual crossing places were impossible—they could never get the Prince past the soldiers guarding them.

Not for the first time luck was with them. As they skirted Loch Skiport on Uist's east coast they ran into four friends of Neil's. They had a boat as they had come to do some fishing and they readily agreed to take Neil, Felix and Charles over to the island of Wiay close to the Benbecula shore. Neil had hoped that his brother would be there to help them, but there was no-one so the fishermen took them the rest of the way and landed them on the Benbecula shore.

By this time it was daylight and the three men had been on the move all night. Charles lay down and fell fast asleep and his friends soon did the same. They could not proceed to Rossinish anyway until after dark.

By nightfall a wind had risen and there was heavy rain. It was a nightmarish tramp over rough moorland. All three kept falling in the dark and losing their shoes in the bogs.

It was a huge relief when, at last, after midnight, they found themselves outside the cottage at Rossinish. Inside they expected to find Flora, Lady Clanranald and a warm welcome. Still, it was best to be cautious. The Prince and Felix waited a little distance away while Neil knocked on the door. It was opened by the couple who lived in the cottage. There was no Flora, no Lady Clanranald. In a low voice the man of the house told him that twenty soldiers had arrived a couple of days earlier and were sleeping in a tent only a few hundred yards away. It was too dangerous for Flora to come here, or for the Prince and his friends to shelter in the cottage.

It was a desperately anxious moment. They dared not bring the Prince into the house, but a hiding place had to be found somewhere. At any second one of the soldiers camped nearby might wander over and see them standing in the doorway.

A cow-herd lodged with the couple and he came to the rescue. He had a bothy not too far away. It was just a rough little place but it was dry and the three were welcome to shelter in it overnight. Gratefully they accepted. He led them to it. It was a poor resting place compared to what they had hoped for, but they were glad to have it.

In the morning Charles was awake early, impatient as always. Before dawn had properly broken he had seen Felix off to Nunton to find out what Flora was doing and what her plan was now.

No sooner was Felix away than the woman from the house hurried to the bothy to warn them that it would not be safe to stay there any longer. Once the soldiers started moving about some of them might well look into the bothy.

It was raining heavily again, but there was nothing else for it. Charles and Neil slipped down to the shore and spent a miserable day crouching amongst the rocks. There was little shelter from the rain or the midges which attacked them in hordes.

In the evening a messenger came from Nunton with food and drink sent by Lady Clanranald and word that it would be safe enough to move closer to Nunton. They did so and spent the night in the open on beds of heather which Neil made up in the traditional island way.

Their next stopping place was on a hill overlooking Nunton. From here they could watch any comings and goings. Two cousins of Flora's brought them the news that the boat to take them to Skye was now ready. Even better, most of the Government troops on Benbecula had been withdrawn leaving mostly men who were in the militia but secret Jacobite sympathisers.

Felix had returned, so Neil left Charles with him and went down the hill to Lady Clanranald's fine Nunton home. There he learned there had been an unexpected hitch. Charles was six foot tall and the ladies had been unable to lay their hands on any woman's clothes to fit him! The Clanranald servants had been called on to make some specially for him. Now at last they were ready and there was quite a party waiting to go with Charles to Skye: Flora, of course, and Lady Clanranald, her brother Angus and his wife, and Lady Clanranald's seven-year-old daughter Peggy. Neil, too, was to accompany them.

They wasted no time but made their way to the boat and went aboard. The crew of five were ready. They at once cast off and headed round the north tip of Benbecula to Rossinish.

There Charles and Neil welcomed them ashore. Because it was thought there were no longer enemy troops on the island a celebration meal had been prepared in the bothy. All had sat down and were just starting to eat when a friendly herd boy rushed in with the news that well over a thousand soldiers had returned to Benbecula and landed at Nunton.

The party snatched up any food they could carry away and ran down to the boat. It would be too dangerous to set out across the open water to Skye. Instead they headed over Loch Usquevaugh and landed on the far shore in the early morning. Here, in the cold dawn, they ate what they had rescued from the table.

There was always someone ready to carry news. This time it was a servant from Nunton. His news was startling. The troops had taken over Lady Clanranald's home. One of them had actually slept in her empty bed! And even more soldiers were said to be about to invade the island.

Lady Clanranald left at once to go back to Nunton, with her daughter, brother and sister-in-law. The time had come for Charles to don his disguise. He changed clothes in the heather with Flora's help. He had to wear some form of hat which he evidently found most uncomfortable. Here is how Neil described what happened:

'The Prince, stripped of his own clothes, was dressed by Miss Flora in his new attire, but could not keep his hands from adjusting his head-dress, which he cursed a thousand times. The white blue-sprigged gown was of calico, a light coloured quilted petticoat, a mantle of dull camlet made after the Irish fashion, with a cap to cover His Royal Highness's whole head and face, with a suitable head-dress, shoes and stockings.'

Charles had two pistols which he wanted to hide on his person but Flora would not let him. If they were searched, she said, and the pistols found, suspicions would immediately be aroused.

Charles pointed out that if he was searched they would find more than the two pistols! He argued in vain. Flora's mind was made up. She put her foot down, too, when Charles wanted to take both Neil and Felix. They had shared many adventures over the past weeks and he had great trust in them.

Flora would not hear of it. She had three passes, one for herself, one for 'Betty Burke' and one for Neil. She was not going to risk taking Felix without a pass and anyway he sounded too foreign. He must stay behind.

At 8 o'clock in the evening they sailed for Skye. They had chosen their time well: there was not an enemy ship in sight. Their own boat was quite small with a mast and oars. To begin with there was no wind so the crew had to row. The tune of 'The Skye Boat Song' is said to imitate the beat of the oars as they swung in and out of the water:

> 'Speed, bonnie boat, like a bird on the wing
> Over the sea to Skye:
> Carry the lad who is born to be King
> Over the sea to Skye.'

Equally it can be said to suggest the skimming of a small craft across the waves. And for a time she did, for a favourable wind arose at about midnight, but later a mist came down and it began to rain. Visibility was poor. The crewmen stopped rowing and began to quarrel amongst themselves as to which direction they should be taking.

Charles took the situation lightly and sang one patriotic Jacobite song after another while Flora, despite all the noise, was so tired that she fell asleep on the bottom of the boat.

With daybreak, the mist cleared and they found themselves off the coast of Skye. This cheered everyone up until, as they passed Vaternish Point, they saw a party of Government troops watching them. Next moment a shot whistled past the boat and some of the soldiers ran up to a house as if to report what they had seen. No boat was launched to follow them, however, and they went on along the coast until they came to a secluded inlet where they pulled in for a rest and to eat bread they had brought with them.

They had thought that Skye would be safer than Benbecula but were soon to find this was not the case. They had already been fired at even before they had landed although the soldiers could not have known who they were.

Flora's plan now was to contact a friend, Lady Margaret MacDonald, who lived at Mugstot. The boat was moored as close as possible to the house and Flora and Neil went ashore. Before they reached the house they were met by Lady Margaret's maid who told them that her mistress already had several visitors including Lieutenant MacLeod of the Skye militia and four of his men. Other soldiers were in the vicinity.

However, Flora was not to be put off. She went on to the house and asked to see her friend. Lady Margaret was as keen a Jacobite as herself and she was thrilled to hear that Charles was so near. Had it been possible she would gladly have welcomed him into her home. Obviously she couldn't, but, though she was extremely nervous of being found out, she wanted to give what help she could.

As she consulted with others in the household, Flora, cool as ever, chatted to Lieutenant MacLeod in the dining-room. She could have handled the situation better if Lady Margaret had not kept popping in anxiously on feeble excuses to make sure everything was alright!

Afterwards Flora and Neil were told what had been decided. Charles would be safer on the island of Raasay. If they tried to take him there by boat it would mean passing close to a military outpost. They could not hope to pass it unobserved. Instead, Lady Margaret's factor was to guide Charles and Neil on foot across Skye to Portree and sail from there. The Prince would have to continue to wear his woman's clothes for a while yet.

The factor's house was on the route and he was to put them up for the night, so they set off to get there as quickly as they could. It was a Sunday evening and they met streams of churchgoers who turned and stared at the ungainly 'woman' striding along with the two men.

Flora made up on them, riding on a pony, and escorted by a Mrs MacDonald and a maid. The maid knew nothing of what was going on and was amazed by this tall, clumsy person who hitched up her petticoats in a most inelegant manner when there were burns to cross. Flora told her she was an Irishwoman and to take no notice, and Neil, though amused, whispered to Charles to be more careful what he was doing or he would give the game away.

Charles seems to have been a poor actor, convincing no-one, for when they got to the factor's house and his daughter went to tell her mother they had visitors she told her, 'my father has brought in a very old, muckle, ill-shaken-up wife as ever I saw!'

Her mother went to meet the stranger who bent to kiss her hand. As he did so she felt the bristles of his beard and sprang back, going instantly to her husband to demand to know who this peculiar person could be.

'Why, my dear, it is the Prince,' he smiled. 'You have the honour to have him in your house.'

'The Prince!' she cried. 'Then we are all ruined and undone for ever. We will all be hanged!'

'Well,' said her husband, 'we will die but once, and if we are hanged for this, I am sure we die in a good cause.'

He told her to prepare a meal for their guests, which she willingly did.

A good, civilised meal and a proper bed to sleep in—it must have been sheer luxury for the Prince. He slept late next morning and it was well into the day before Flora went to his room to help him, for the last time, into his Betty Burke costume. He was heard playing the fool with her, crying out in a woman's voice, 'Oh, Miss, you have forgot my apron! Where is my apron?'

Flora and Neil rode ahead to Portree to await his arrival there. Charles could not take the same busy route but was led over the hills by quiet cattle paths. Soon after they set out, they stopped in a wood and Charles was at last able to take off his disguise and put on the kilt, jacket and plaid to which he had become accustomed since arriving in Scotland. He must have been glad of the change for it started to rain again and he got soaked on the rest of the journey.

His Betty Burke clothes were hidden in the wood but someone returned later and burned them, all except the blue-sprigged cotton gown. It was eventually taken to Edinburgh and the design was copied by a dress-maker and became fashionable wear amongst Jacobite ladies.

It was thought safe enough in Portree to take Charles to an inn, where he was lent a dry kilt and shirt and he enjoyed the warmth of a roaring fire. It was only a short break, though, for soon, out in the darkness, there came a knock on the door and the muttered message that the boat was waiting to take him to Raasay.

Before he went aboard he said goodbye to Flora and Neil MacEachain. He owed them both a lot and he knew it. To Flora he said, 'For all that has happened, I hope we shall meet at St James's yet' (St James's Palace was then the London home of the royal family). He promised her he would reward her for what she had done.

She and Neil watched the boat slip silently away. It was soon out of sight in the dark.

Two more months were to pass before Charles escaped from

Scotland and returned to France. Months in which he went through more adventures and had further narrow escapes from capture. He was to be back on Skye again and in various hiding places in the Highlands.

He was never able to reward Flora or any of the brave people who risked their lives to help him, for he was to spend the rest of his life in exile on the Continent. There is a story that, long years later, he crossed secretly to London to gaze on St James's Palace from the outside and to think on what might have been. It is said he took a look at the Tower of London, too, for it was there he would have been imprisoned and possibly beheaded had he been caught at the time of the '45 Uprising.

As for all the Scots who had helped him, many suffered heavy punishment for their 'crimes', as did their families. They lost their homes, their lands, many their lives.

The man who had defeated the Jacobites at Culloden, 'Butcher' Cumberland as he became known, took a terrible revenge on the Highlands, a revenge which virtually destroyed the old clan system and traditional way of life.

Neil was lucky. He escaped to France and returned to military life, serving as an officer in the French army.

Flora was arrested and spent months in the Tower of London, but after she was released she fell in love and married, emigrating with her husband to North Carolina. Her husband fought in the American War of Independence. After some years the couple returned to Scotland. She had ten children to whom she no doubt told, many times, the story of Betty Burke, the maid she had once had, who was really a Prince in disguise.

There is no evidence, though, that she ever thought of herself as a heroine or as having done anything particularly brave, and she would probably be amazed to know how her name has lived on in Scotland. She would be astonished, too, to see the fine statue of herself outside the castle of Inverness. It is one of the few major statues erected in memory of a woman in Scotland.

Brainwave on Glasgow Green

(1765)

There is a famous engraving which used to appear in school books. It showed the inventor James Watt as a boy sitting in his mother's kitchen staring intently at the steam lifting the lid of the kettle on the stove.

Many people grew up believing that this showed a true historical incident—the discovery of steam power. But of course it did not happen like that at all. He was almost 30 when he got the idea which led to the widespread use of the steam engine as a source of power.

Born in Greenock, James made an unpromising start in life. He was sickly, shy, and not very bright at school. However, his father noticed that he was good with his hands and he encouraged his son to develop his skills in a workshop in the attic.

James spent most of his time up there, becoming ever more ambitious in the things he turned out: pumps, pulleys, a small crane, even a barrel-organ.

He might have gone to university, but the early death of his mother and a shortage of money to feed and clothe the rest of the family meant he had to go out and fend for himself.

He went to London and trained as an instrument-maker, work which was not at all difficult for a young man already used to constructing quite complicated objects.

Then he returned to Glasgow and very soon was running his own business making and repairing instruments in a workshop in the grounds of the University.

Later he moved to larger premises, took a partner and a number of assistants, and branched out into making and repairing toys and musical instruments.

It was when the University asked him to mend its model steam engine that he got his great idea. Steam engines at that time were in great demand for pumping water from coal mines. They were primitive contraptions, however, and not very efficient. Taking the University model to pieces and re-assembling it gave Watt the notion of building a much better one. But how?

On a historic Sunday afternoon in 1765 he went for a walk on Glasgow Green, pondering his problem. Here is how he described what happened: 'It was in the Green of Glasgow, I had gone to take a walk on a fine Sabbath afternoon. I had entered the Green by the gate at the foot of Charlotte Street—had passed to the old washing-house. I was thinking upon the engine at the time, and gone so far as the Herd's house when the idea came into my mind that, as steam is an elastic body, it would rush into a vacuum, and if communication were made between the cylinder and an exhausted vessel, it would rush into it, and might then be condensed without cooling the cylinder.'

The University steam engine, like others of its day, could drive a pump and that was all. The condensation of the steam which powered the engine was achieved by the clumsy method of sending a jet of cold water into the cylinder. By adding a separate chamber for the condensation, Watt was able to prevent the main cylinder from losing heat. As a result, steam engines could have far more power than anyone had believed possible.

This was the break-through point. From it James Watt went on to make other improvements to the steam engine so that it could power large machines at low cost. Problems arose about manufacturing his sophisticated engine. Unable to get it made in Scotland he moved south, to Birmingham, where a new partner, Matthew Boulton, ran a huge ironworks.

There was a lot of luck in Watt's life as well as hard work and mechanical genius. Boulton was a clever businessman, which Watt was not. Without Boulton's good business sense, he might never have enjoyed the fruits of success. Watt knew this and appreciated all that Boulton did for him.

He never lost his enquiring mind and was experimenting and trying out new ideas to the end of his life when he died, honoured as one of the great minds of his day.

He had, after all, made possible the industrialisation of Britain. The factories that sprang up in the towns and cities were powered by his brain-child, the Watt steam engine. The quiet, sickly boy from Greenock had certainly left his mark.

The inscription on his statue in Westminster Abbey states that, through his steam engine, he 'enlarged the resources of his country, increased the power of men, and rose to an eminent place among the most illustrious followers of science and the real benefactors of the world.'

The Dark Deeds of Deacon Brodie

(1787-1788)

One Sunday in 1787 an Edinburgh lady decided she did not feel well enough to go to church. As she sat in her parlour, she was astonished to see the door open and a man walk in. He was smartly dressed but the lower half of his face was covered by a silk cloth.

Calmly he picked up the bunch of keys lying on the table in front of her, opened her desk, took out some money and re-locked the desk. He then walked back to the table, replaced the keys, bowed low, and then left the room as quietly as he had come in. The lady sat amazed. She realised she had just been burgled, and what is more, she was certain she knew the intruder. 'That was Deacon Brodie!' she exclaimed.

Although she was so sure, she did not report the theft. Who would believe her? Everybody would say she must have been dreaming! William Brodie was a highly-respected business man. He was a cabinet-maker, in other words he made furniture, and the fact he had been chosen to be a deacon meant he was a master of his craft. He was a popular figure, well-known for his good humour. How could such a man possibly be a thief?

The strange thing was that Old Edinburgh had been hit recently by a whole string of robberies. Shops and houses had been broken into and goods and money stolen. Even a gold mace had been taken from one of the colleges. It looked like the work of a well-organised gang for they left no clues behind them. No-one, up till now, had seen anything of the robbers, and no-one, decided the lady, would believe her if she spoke out.

Yet she was quite right. The leader of the robber gang was indeed Deacon Brodie. By day he worked hard, running his business, respected by one and all. But when night came he met up with a group of unsavoury cronies to plot the next robbery. With his knowledge of homes and businesses in the city he knew when and where to strike.

Of course it all had to end. Sooner or later the gang would go too far. It was Brodie himself who brought about their downfall. One day one of his more respectable friends mentioned that he was making a business call at the Excise Office in Chessell's Court. Brodie went along, too, and imediately he began to plan a break-in. He found excuses to return several times alone or with one of his gang, an Englishman called George Smith, and each time he studied the lay-out of the offices, until he knew exactly how to break in and lay hands on the money.

At last, on one of his visits, he managed to steal the key to the outer door, made a copy, and returned the original to its hook.

Now he was ready. On the evening of 5 March 1788, Brodie, Smith, and two others, John Brown and Andrew Ainsley, met at Smith's house. Brodie was the last to arrive. He was in great good spirits, and he had a pistol in his belt which he drew out and flourished as he sang them a song:

> 'Let us take the road!
> Hark, hark, I hear the sound of coaches!
> The hour of attack approaches,
> To your arms, brave boys and load!'

They ate a meal of herrings and chicken and then set out to the Excise Office. Brodie had told them his plan. He would unlock the main door. Brown was to keep watch by the railings outside while Brodie would do the same inside the doorway. Smith and Ainsley were to go inside and break open the door of the cashier's room. If either Brown or Brodie saw someone approaching from the street they were to blow one blast on a whistle. If there was more than one person they were to give three blasts.

There was a slight change of plan because the porter was seen leaving the Excise building and Brodie told Brown to follow him and make sure he went home, then to return. When Brown came back, Ainsley had taken his post at the railings so he went inside with Smith.

The two got into the cashier's office but, despite opening several cupboards and drawers, did not find as much cash as they had hoped. After a search lasting about half an hour, they heard a sound and hurried to leave. To their alarm, Brodie and Ainsley had both disappeared. These two later claimed that they had seen a man come running down the court and they had blown a warning blast on their whistles before slipping away. If they did so, Smith and Brown never heard them.

The four thieves met some evenings later and divided the spoils between them, but by this time Brown was thoroughly unnerved. There was a huge public outcry about this latest robbery and the police were pulling out all the stops to trace the culprits. Next day Brown went to the police and confessed. By promising to testify against the others in court, he hoped to escape punishment. Ainsley, too, decided to try to save his skin by giving evidence against Brodie.

Brodie, however, was not going to be captured so easily. By the time the police went to arrest him he had left Edinburgh. A King's messenger was sent in pursuit and he followed Brodie's trail to Dunbar, then Newcastle, and then London. From there Brodie crossed the Channel in disguise and took refuge in Amsterdam.

He might never have been found had he not sent letters to three friends in Edinburgh. These were opened by the British Consul in Ostend who at once arranged for Brodie to be arrested and sent back to Scotland to face justice. True to form, on the journey home, Brodie entertained the King's messenger and other passengers with hilarious tales of exploits he had enjoyed in Amsterdam.

Edinburgh was swept with a fever of excitement when the trial of Brodie and Smith opened at the High Court on 27 August. The revelation that a set of keys for opening lock-fast premises had been found in Brodie's Lawnmarket office, as well as other evidence against him, shocked all decent citizens. In vain Brodie tried to prove an alibi for the night of the Excise robbery. With Brown and Ainsley testifying against him, it was hopeless. He and Smith were condemned to be hanged.

Around 40,000 people gathered to watch the scene. Brodie was in good spirits to the end while Smith looked downcast and forlorn as he had throughout the trial. At the foot of the gallows Brodie clapped Smith on the shoulder, saying, 'George Smith, you're first in hand!'

Smith mounted the gallows slowly and reluctantly but the bold Brodie marched up briskly and examined the rope. He insisted that it be readjusted three times before he was satisfied. But then he would have known whether it was correct or not, for the gallows on which he died had been constructed to his own design!

Just over 50 years later, Robert Louis Stevenson was born in Edinburgh. Of course he was to hear all about the dark deeds of Deacon Brodie. They appealed to his writer's imagination and it is believed that *The Strange Case Of Dr Jekyll And Mr Hyde* was partly inspired by Brodie's story. The novel deals with a good, kind doctor who, when he takes a certain drug, turns into a cruel and ruthless fiend. He is a man whose face of respectability is only a mask that hides his other evil self—just like William Brodie.

An Amazing Dinner Party
(1847)

If you had been outside a certain house in Queen Street, Edinburgh, on an evening in November 1847, you would have seen several guests roll up in their horse-drawn carriages. Inside, the lamps were lit, the table was set for dinner.

The host was James Simpson, a clever young doctor who for several years had been Professor of Midwifery at the city's University.

As a working doctor he had delivered countless babies and he knew well the pain that women suffered in childbirth. He had long searched for some means of saving them that pain, so far without success.

He was certain that some form of drug was the answer, an anaesthetic that would dull the patient's senses, even put them to sleep for a time. But what? He had tried sulphuric ether and it had worked. However, it had a horrible smell, irritated the lungs and left patients ill for days.

All of which delighted the many in the medical profession who were bitterly opposed to any form of anaesthetic. They considered the idea unnatural and dangerous and they thought men like Simpson were a disgrace to medicine. They thought nothing of amputating arms and legs without relieving the pain in any way, and they took for granted that their patients would scream in agony on the operating table until they fell into a merciful faint.

Simpson did not care what they said. He continued to search for a safe and suitable drug. Recently he had been sent, from Liverpool, a new, untried product called chloroform. Tonight he was going to try it out.

The dinner party was, to begin with, just like any other, but amongst the guests were Simpson's two assistants, both doctors, and they alone knew what was going to happen.

When the meal was finished and the table cleared, the experiment began. Simpson laid out several different drugs and, as his guests watched in some amazement, the three men started to sniff them one by one.

The drugs had very little effect and soon they had used them all. Only the small bottle of chloroform sat unopened. Simpson reached for it and drew the cork. He poured a little into three tumblers and they picked them up and inhaled.

The aroma was sweet and pleasant and the result almost instant. The three men said how nice it was, how good they felt, and then— crash! Simpson slid under the table, closely followed by his assistants. The three were in a deep sleep, one of them snoring loudly.

The guests stared in consternation. They did not know what to do. But they did not have long to wait. The three slumberers awoke and got to their feet none the worse. Soon they were delightedly shaking hands with one another, congratulating themselves on the results. The experiment had been a success beyond their wildest hopes.

James Simpson had to fight hard to convince his profession that chloroform was the answer for operations. It took years to break down the barriers of prejudice and distrust.

Fortunately Queen Victoria believed in what Simpson was doing. She made him one of her Physicians in Scotland and in 1853 she asked him to administer chloroform to her for the birth of Prince Leopold.

That put the seal of respectability on anaesthetics and finally opened the door to their general use.

Simpson's career went from strength to strength. He was constantly introducing improvements for the benefit of patients and he received a knighthood for the great work he had done.

When he died a statue was raised to him in Princes Street Gardens and there is a plaque on what was his home at 52 Queen Street, where he held that amazing and historic dinner party.

Baird's Magic Eye

(1925)

John Logie Baird started experimenting early. In the garden of his home in Helensburgh on the Clyde, with the help of a school friend, he built an aeroplane. It consisted mostly of two box kites joined together. But he reckoned it would glide and had it hoisted up on to the roof of the house.

He climbed in, his friend pushed him off and he was launched into the air. Unfortunately the contraption broke in two and he fell to the lawn.

He never flew again.

At 13 he had devised his own telephone system with lines criss-crossing the street, linking him up with his friends. This was going well until one night a low wire caught an old man round the neck and nearly strangled him.

He turned to electric lighting, then in its infancy. The local paper reported that the Baird home 'was now enjoying electric light, thanks to the ingenuity of a young member of the household.' He had done it by purchasing a second-hand oil engine and building a dynamo.

After school John went to the Royal Technical College, Glasgow, and then took a job as an electrical supply engineer. He left because of ill health and boredom and started to think up a whole series of inventions.

There was a cure for haemorrhoids (piles), a medicated undersock, synthetic diamonds, glass razor-blades, pneumatic shoes, and other things best forgotten. For a time he left Scotland for Trinidad where he made jams and chutneys. His premises were over-run by insects which found their way into everything and he sailed for home with what stock could be rescued.

In 1924 he settled in Hastings on the Sussex Coast. Perhaps it reminded him of Helensburgh. It was here he began to grapple with the problems of sending pictures by wire. A German inventor had made an early attempt to do this but had not got very far. Baird worked on the idea using whatever materials were to hand: a tea chest, hat box, darning needles, sealing wax, transformers, wires and batteries. The wonder is that it worked. One great day he succeeded in transmitting the silhouette of a cardboard Maltese Cross.

He pressed on to improve his methods, but it all nearly came to an end when, touching live wires, he was thrown off his feet by a powerful current. Luckily he broke the circuit as he crashed to the floor.

He was renting a property at the time and the owner was sure that the mad Scotsman would one day blow the place to bits. He ordered him out.

Baird moved to London and continued his experiments in an attic in Frith Street, Soho. The proprietor of a big store became interested in what he was doing and invited him to give a public demonstration. Customers who had gone in to buy clothes quickly queued up to gaze at shapes transmitted through a piece of flex a few yards in length.

Baird knew he was making progress, but there was still more work to be done. He kept on experimenting. In his makeshift laboratory he kept a dummy which he called Bill. Time and time again he tried different methods of showing it on his 'viewing box'. It could nearly always be seen but only as a rather fuzzy shape. Then one day, as he tinkered with the transmitter, it all fell into place. He switched on and there in the viewing box was Bill, every feature of him crisp and clear, the eyes, the nose, the mouth.

In high excitement Baird rushed downstairs and burst into the office below.

The office boy was sorting envelopes. Baird dragged him upstairs, pushed Bill out of the chair and sat the boy in his place. 'Sit still—that's all. Just sit still!' He dashed to the transmitter in the next room. The screen was blank. What had gone wrong? He rushed back and found the boy was shrinking away from the lights and the heat.

Baird pleaded with him to put up with the discomfort, slipped him some money he could ill afford and hurried to the other room. On the screen was a clear picture of the boy's face, indignant, a little frightened. He didn't understand what was going on, didn't realise he was the first person in the world ever to be televised.

He was also the second person in history to see television, for Baird insisted on sitting on the chair himself and sending the boy through to the other room to look at the screen.

The boy was not impressed and quickly made his getaway back down to his envelopes.

That day in 1925 should have been the beginning of great things for John Logie Baird. It wasn't. True, he held a successful demonstration of his invention before a large gathering of scientists the following year. He also received help from the BBC in proving that pictures could be sent a long distance. And he formed the very first television company, the first licensed station.

He was a poor businessman, however, and made little money from his 'magic eye' as the newspapers of the day called it. Other men reaped the benefits of his genius and for a time he was almost forgotten as the television industry grew and flourished.

Now, though, he is rightly given his deserved place as the Father of Television.

He died in 1946 and his body was taken back to Helensburgh, where it all started and where he lies in a cemetery above the Clyde.

The Stone Comes Home

(1950-51)

It was Christmas-time in London. With just two days to go the streets were thronged with shoppers. Mingling with them were four young Scots who had driven down from Glasgow the night before. Buying Christmas presents was the last thing on their minds.

In the late afternoon they left the crowded streets and strolled, in pairs, into Westminster Abbey. In the huge dim building they made their way past the many monuments to the Chapel of Edward the Confessor. There stood the Coronation Chair and, beneath it, the Stone of Destiny.

After studying it for several minutes they turned to go, pausing to gaze at the Tomb of Edward I, the man who had brought the Stone to London 700 years before.

He had seized it from the Abbey at Scone, Perthshire, where it had been used in the crowning ceremonies of Scotland's monarchs. Robert the Bruce himself had sat upon it when he was crowned.

Even earlier, long before Scotland was a nation, it had been the coronation seat in the Kingdom of Dalriada in what is now the West of Scotland.

But there is an even older tradition connected with it. In the Bible the story is told of Jacob going on a journey and lying down to sleep one night, with a stone as a pillow. In his sleep he dreamed he saw a ladder reaching up to Heaven and angels going up and down. He then heard the voice of God.

In the morning, before he continued on his journey, Jacob set up the stone as a sacred object.

Later the stone was carried away and cherished by wandering tribes. From the Holy Land it was taken, over several generations, through Sicily, Spain and Ireland, until it came to rest in Dalriada. From there it was a shorter journey to Scone. By 1296, when Edward, in a fit of temper, carried off the Stone, it was regarded, because of its history, as one of Scotland's most priceless relics. Edward was well aware of this and by stealing it he hoped to demonstrate his power and crush Scottish hopes of independence from England.

Since its arrival in London the Stone had been kept beneath the English Coronation Chair and all the kings and queens of the United Kingdom had been crowned sitting over it. From time to time, though, the question was asked in Scotland, 'Why must it stay in London? Why can't it be returned to its rightful home north of the Border?' Many Scots felt that because it had been taken by Edward without permission it ought to be handed back.

The four young visitors to the Abbey that winter afternoon shared that view. That is why, instead of getting ready to enjoy Christmas like everyone else, they had hired a car and come to London with one simple but breathtaking aim: to bring the Stone of Scone home to Scotland!

Ian Hamilton was the ringleader. Although he was a student of Law at the University of Glasgow he was prepared to break the law, he felt so strongly on the matter.

He had recruited three people to help him. Kay Mathieson had just started work as a teacher of Domestic Science, while Gavin Vernon and his friend Alan Stuart were both students. Ian had fired them with his own enthusiasm, his sense of injustice.

He had been to the Abbey on an earlier trip to London, when he had studied the lie of the land: the visit the four made that afternoon was to let the others see the position of the Stone and to plan its route out of the building. One of the first obstacles they noted was the six wooden steps leading out of the Confessor's Chapel. They were narrow and steep, while the Stone looked heavier and bigger than Ian remembered it.

Before they tackled the steps they would have to ease the Stone out from its tight fit beneath the Coronation Chair.

Once they had it out and down the steps they would have to carry it to one of the exit doors. The Stone has a large iron ring at either end which might come in useful there.

After their visit to the Abbey the four friends held a council-of-war in a cafe. Would they wait until the next night, which was Christmas Eve, or strike tonight? Kay made up their minds for them. She did not want to stay a moment longer in London than she had to. 'Let's get on with it,' she said and the others agreed.

They all knew what they had to do. Ian was to enter the Abbey shortly before closing time, find a place to hide and wait till the building was locked up for the night. He would then open a door for the others to come in and help carry the Stone to the car. A second car had been hired and the four were to split up. Alan and Kay were to take the Stone and drive out of London to the West. They all reckoned the Police would not be expecting the Stone to be taken in that direction but would be concentrating their watch on the roads to Scotland. Even if Ian and Gavin were stopped as they drove North, there would be nothing in their car to connect them with the taking of the Stone.

While Kay and Alan went to rehearse their escape route out of London, Ian and Gavin drove to the Embankment by the Thames and parked the car. Here Ian took from his bag the tools he might need for his night's work: a jemmy, a file, a saw, a wrench, a torch. They were strange tools for a student of Law! He stowed them into his pockets, put on his coat to hide them and was ready to return to the Abbey.

Gavin drove to a shadowed spot near the building and Ian climbed out of the car—rather stiffly because of all he was carrying—and walked through the doorway as 5.15 boomed from Big Ben.

He strolled down one of the aisles, doing his best to look like an ordinary visitor. An elderly guide was chatting to a woman, but they took no notice of Ian and he was soon out of sight amongst the monuments and pillars. He knew exactly where he was going. In a dark corner he had earlier noticed a cleaner's trolley. It was high enough off the floor for him to crawl under. He slipped below and lay still.

The stone floor was cold and uncomfortable and it seemed a long time till he heard six o'clock strike. That was the Abbey's closing time and everybody, visitors and staff, should now have left. He waited 15 minutes and then poked his head out cautiously. The lights were out.

He was not due to let the others in for some time but he had had enough of the cold, hard floor and decided to find another hiding place. Slipping out from under the trolley he took off his shoes and began to pad down the aisle.

He had gone only a short way when there was a jingle of keys and a torch shone full on him. There in front of him stood a night-watchman. It would be difficult to say which of them got the bigger shock.

'What the devil are you doing here?' the man demanded.

'I've been shut in,' said Ian, which was true.

The man stared at Ian's stockinged feet, the shoes in his hands.

'I was frightened someone would hear me,' Ian explained.

The man told him to put on his shoes. As Ian bent to do so, he could feel the various tools about his body slip dangerously. If the jemmy was to clatter to the floor now...

'Have you any money?' the man asked, a kindlier note in his voice.

Ian nodded.

'Well, if you're sure you weren't sheltering because you had nowhere else to go...'

Ian assured him that was not why he was there. The man led him to the door, unlocked it and showed him out. 'Merry Christmas,' he called after him. 'Merry Christmas,' said Ian and hurried out gratefully.

He felt a real fool as he plodded away. The others had driven off to pass the hours till it was time to return to the Abbey. There was no saying where they were now. Ian's steps led him to the Embankment. He could hardly believe his luck when he saw Gavin's car parked there. Gavin was not in it and Ian had no key, but he did not have too long to wait.

Gavin, strolling up, stared in amazement.

'Get inside and I'll tell you,' said Ian.

Sitting in the car, Ian explained what had happened. Gavin said it could have been worse: the man might have turned him over to the police.

Ian had to agree. He felt grateful to the watchman for his kindness, and guilty that he had had to deceive him. He hoped the man would not get into trouble after tonight was all over.

They drove the short distance to the place where Gavin had arranged to meet Kay and Alan after their exploration of the route to the West.

When they had all had a meal they held another council-of-war. The result was that they drove near the Abbey several times that night considering if there was any way in. In the end they parked the two cars close to the Albert Hall and slept in them till morning.

It was now Christmas Eve. They had baths at one of the stations and mingled with the crowds in Westminster Abbey.

They had decided it would be too risky for Ian, or any of them, to try hiding again in the Abbey. With that out, the only other answer was to force one of the doors. There was one near the Poets' Corner which seemed ideal. It was approached by a little lane. There was a locked gate on the lane but there was also a side door through a hoarding which would take them past workmens' huts to a point beyond the gate and close to the door they were targeting.

All that day Kay felt more and more ill. She confided in Ian. 'I'm terribly sorry. I think I've got flu.' She was white and shivering. There was only one thing for it: she took a room in a small hotel to get a few hours' rest while the others put time in as best they could in the crowded streets. For them the day seemed endless.

At last, at two o'clock on the morning of Christmas Day, Ian, Alan and Gavin approached the door in the hoarding. There was a padlock on it but it opened easily. They passed through it and ran up to the Poets' Corner door.

Now that they knew they could reach it they quickly turned away and slipped back on to the street, arranging the padlock on the hoarding door so that it looked as if it was still locked.

Next thing to do was to collect Kay from her hotel. It took some thumping on the door before the proprietor woke up and let them in, but at last Kay was with them in the car, still under the weather, but determined to play her part.

Back at the Abbey, parked in a dark lane, she waited in the driving seat while the others made their way through the shadows to the Poets' Corner door. It took the combined strength of all three to force it open. At every creak they expected a rush of feet from inside or the screech of a police car outside.

The door flew open with a crash and they waited, listening. Nothing. They followed one another inside and Ian closed the door behind them. Ahead they could see some lights but much of the interior was in darkness. Ian was glad he had brought his torch. They went quickly and quietly to the Chapel of Edward the Confessor. Ian shone the torch full on the Coronation Chair and the Stone beneath it.

They went up to it. There was a thin piece of wood in front of the Stone which would have to be removed. It came away easily, but even with that out of the way it was no easy thing to pull the Stone out. It was, as Ian had suspected, a tight fit in the narrow space under the chair. The rings at either end kept catching. The three friends pulled, and pulled again.

At last the Stone slid out and landed with a bump on the floor. 'A coat,' said somebody. Ian threw off his and they shifted the stone on to it. There must have been a fault in the stone for as Ian lifted one end by the ring, about a quarter of the slab broke off. He lifted it up and, heavy though it was, ran with it to the door and out to the waiting car. Kay saw him coming and was ready. In a moment it was lying on the back seat.

Ian took a deep breath and hurried back into the Abbey where Alan and Gavin were struggling with the dead weight in Ian's coat. Fortunately it was a well-made coat otherwise it would have ripped under the strain. As it was, although there were tearing noises, it held all the way to the outer door.

It was then things went wrong. As they opened the door they were shocked to hear the car engine starting up and the car move

The Stone of Destiny in Westminster Abbey

off. Without a word, Ian shut the door on the others and rushed out to see what was happening. The car had stopped a little way along and as he got inside beside Kay he saw why she had moved—there was a policeman approaching. By the time he reached the car Ian had thrown a spare coat over the Stone and he and Kay were kissing as though they were sweethearts. They broke apart as the policeman greeted them. Full of the Christmas spirit he chatted in a friendly manner. He advised Kay that she was not parked in an ideal place and would be better to drive to a nearby car park. It was one they knew well already for the other car was waiting there. Thanking him they drove off, hoping Alan and Gavin would keep out of sight until they returned.

In the car park they hastily discussed their next move. It seemed best now to split up and for Kay to drive the smaller piece of stone to safety. Ian would return to the Abbey to deal with the situation there.

He remained in the car to guide her for several streets, then he jumped out, waved her goodbye and started back on foot. When he reached the Abbey, things were strangely quiet. The Stone lay where they had left it, but there was no sign of Gavin and Alan. Later, when Ian found them again, he heard what had happened. They had seen the policeman talking to Ian and Kay and then the car drive off. Just after that a police car had come tearing along, its siren blaring.

Thinking they were all about to be arrested, they made a run for it and still believed they were being hunted when Ian came on them in a distant street some hours later.

Meantime Ian found himself on his own with the abandoned stone. Could he move it on his own? He had to try. He raced from the Abbey to the car park and then drove back again. Parking by the hoarding he dashed inside, half fearing that the Stone would be gone. It was still there. Somehow he pulled the great slab to the car. He tipped it on end and with a huge effort toppled it into the car. At the end of it all, it seemed so simple. He had done it single-handed! The car sank and creaked under the weight on the back seat but thankfully no damage was done.

A few tense minutes later he was driving over Westminster Bridge, crossing the Thames on his way South. It was before he was clear of the city that he spotted Alan and Gavin hurrying along and gave them the fright of their lives when he drew up beside them with a screech of brakes.

They were amazed and overjoyed when Ian threw open the rear door and lifted a coat to show them what lay there.

'You've got it!' they chorused. 'But how—?'

Later that day the Stone was laid to rest in the lee of a grassy bank in Kent, the first time it had felt fresh country air for hundreds of years. A few nights later it was moved to an even more secluded spot.

The smaller piece of stone, which Kay had taken, spent some time in Birmingham where Kay stayed with a friend before returning home.

The disappearance of the Stone from Westminster Abbey was headline news for weeks on both sides of the Border. In Scotland people talked of little else. There was a nationwide search to recover it and to find and arrest those who had taken it.

Although there were some Scots who condemned what had been done, there were many who sympathised with the unknown group who had done it. There was a feeling that it was something that had to be done and that an ancient wrong had been righted.

A number of Scots knew or suspected some of those involved but none of the four responsible was ever charged and they were able, under the noses of the authorities, to smuggle both parts of the Stone back to Scotland and place them in safe hands. The break was repaired by a skilled stonemason who happened also to be a Glasgow City Councillor. He accepted the task as a huge honour and the highpoint of his life.

However, Ian knew that he could not keep the Stone hidden for too long. Sooner or later the police efforts were going to be successful and he did not want to see good friends suffering embarrassment and perhaps having their careers and lives blighted.

Also the last thing he wanted was for the police to track down the Stone and take it away by force. That would be no way to treat an object dear to the heart of the nation.

With friends he drew up a petition to the King, George VI, explaining why the Stone had been taken and stating firmly that 'its proper place of retention is among His Majesty's Scottish people who, above all, hold this symbol dear.'

The petition promised that the Stone would be handed back if an assurance was given that it would remain in Scotland.

A second petition, on similar lines, was nailed to the door of the High Kirk of St Giles on Edinburgh's historic Royal Mile. There was no response to either request but to Ian it seemed that the best course of action now was to hand back the Stone. He and his friends had proved their point, they had shown what the Stone meant to the people of Scotland. Surely this would be taken to heart?

On 11 April 1951 Ian and two friends took the Stone to the old Abbey of Arbroath, laid it reverently before the High Altar then turned and walked away. They chose Arbroath because it gave its name to the Declaration of Independence of 1320.

The Stone was not kept in Scotland. It was seized by the police and rushed back down to London where, after examination, it was replaced under the Coronation Chair.

It was not to return to Scotland until St Andrew's Day, 1996, when, following a surprise decision by the Government, it was brought back to occupy a place of honour prepared for it in Edinburgh Castle.

Some people still claim that the stone that was handed back at Arbroath was not the real one but a substitute prepared by the Glasgow mason. The experts in England who examined it say that this is untrue, and Ian Hamilton swears that it is the stone he took from Westminster. There is an even older belief that King Edward was deceived back in 1296, and that the true Stone was placed in hiding while a false one was carried in triumph to London. One of the hiding places put forward for the real one is Dunsinane Hill, the scene of Macbeth's great battle. An old local tradition holds that the

Stone of Scone lies there in a secret spot.

Others go back even further and claim that the stone carried out of the Holy Land as a sacred relic was not the real Jacob's Pillow, or at least the stone brought to Dalriada and then Scone could not be it.

It is true, as the historian Nigel Tranter has pointed out, that the Stone of Scone we know today is very shallow and rough and seems an unlikely object ever to have been used in coronations. Anyone sitting on it to be crowned would look very undignified indeed, it is so low. Tranter and other historians maintain that the original Stone of Destiny was higher, shaped like a seat, and decorated with fine carvings.

It is all a mystery and no doubt people will continue to argue over it for a long time to come.

After the events of Christmas 1950, the four who carried out the Abbey raid got on with their lives. Ian Hamilton completed his law studies and became a leading Queen's Counsel who has fought many battles on behalf of clients in the Scottish courts. He has remained a rebel at heart, however, and his outspoken views on many national matters have often been out of tune with those of 'polite' society.

Kay Mathieson became a school teacher in the Highlands and lived quietly until her retirement. Gavin Vernon carved a successful career in the U.S.A. and Alan Stewart went into business and prospered.

None of them ever forgot the stir they caused on that memorable Christmas Eve.

Recommended Reading

(Note: some of these books may be out of print and available only through libraries.)

Theo Aronson, *Kings Over the Water* (London, 1979)

G. W. S. Barrow, *Robert Bruce and the Community of the Realm of Scotland* (Edinburgh, 1988)

Lachlan D. Buchanan, *Stories from Perth's History* (Perth, 1978)

William Creech *An Account of the Trial of William Brodie and George Smith* (Edinburgh, 1788)

Ian Fellowes-Gordon, *Scottish Lives* (London, 1967)

Robert S. Fittis, *Heroines of Scotland* (Paisley, 1889)

Robert Ford, *The Harp of Perthshire* (Paisley, 1893)

Antonia Fraser, *Mary, Queen of Scots* (London, 1971)

Peter and Fiona Somerset Fry, *The History of Scotland* (London, 1985)

Seton Gordon, *Highways and Byways in the West Highlands* (London and Edinburgh, 1995)

Cuthbert Graham, *Portrait of Aberdeen and Deeside* (London, 1980)

Ian Hamilton, *No Stone Unturned* (London, 1953)

Ian Hamilton, *The Taking of the Stone of Destiny* (Moffat, 1991)

W. S. Hanson, *Agricola and the Conquest of the North* (London, 1987)

Paul Hopkins, *Glencoe and the End of the Highland War* (Edinburgh 1986)

Jack House, *Portrait of the Clyde* (London, 1975)

John Kay, *Original Portraits and Caricature Etchings* (London, 1877)

James Kenworthy (Ed.), *Agricola's Campaigns in Scotland* (Edinburgh, 1981)

Magnus Linklater, *Massacre: The Story of Glencoe* (London, 1982)

Magnus Linklater and Christian Hesketh, *John Graham of Claverhouse, Bonnie Dundee* (London and Edinburgh, 1992)

J. D. Mackie, *A History of Scotland* (London, 1978)

R. L. Mackie, *A Short History of Scotland* (Edinburgh, 1978)

Alasdair Maclean and John S. Gibson, *Summer Hunting a Prince* (Stornoway, 1992)

Fitzroy Maclean, *Bonnie Prince Charlie* (London, 1988)

Alexander Maclehose *Historic Haunts of Scotland* (London 1936)

Peter Marren *Grampian Battlefields* (Aberdeen, 1990)

Rosalind K. Marshall, *Queen of Scots* (Edinburgh, 1986)

William Marshall, *Historic Scenes In Perthshire* (Edinburgh, 1881)

Rosalie Masson, *Edinburgh* (London, 1907)

Gordon Maxwell, *A Battle Lost* (Edinburgh, 1990)

Sheriff Rampini, *Tales of Old Scotland* (Edinburgh, 1890)

Anna Ritchie and David J. Breeze, *Invaders of Scotland* (London)

John Sadler, *Scottish Battles*, (Edinburgh, 1996)

Tom Scott, *Tales of Sir William Wallace* (Edinburgh, 1981)

Sir Walter Scott, *Tales of a Grandfather* (Edinburgh, 1828)

Ian G. Smith, *The First Roman Invasion of Scotland* (Edinburgh, 1987)

T. C. Smout, *A History of the Scottish People* (London, 1969)

Alan Spence, *Discovering the Borders* (Edinburgh, 1992)

Elizabeth Sutherland, *In Search of the Picts* (London, 1994)

Nigel Tranter, *Scottish Castles* (Edinburgh, 1982)

Nigel Tranter, *A Traveller's Guide to the Scotland of Robert the Bruce* (London, 1985)

N. H. Walker, *Loch Leven's Royal Prisoner* (Auchterarder, 1983)

Graham Webster, *The Roman Army* (Chester, 1973)